I love this book. Much of what comes through Dalende's friend, Knenesset, could be found in my work as well. Her sincere questions into everyday life and mastery of individuals is easy to read and understand. Many who are discovering their old ways of living and thinking not working will find a special way of being different through the guidance of Knenesset. What exactly is happening in the reality and how do I change my life? Find this answer and more in *Conversations with a Friend*.

Maureen J. St. Germain, Mystic, teacher and
Author of *Beyond the Flower of Life*.

Conversations with a Friend

Dalende (Gelma Bruce)

BALBOA.
PRESS
A DIVISION OF HAY HOUSE

Images created by Anna D. Bruce-Sweetser (www.annadbruce.com).

Balboa Press books may be ordered through booksellers or by contacting:

ISBN:978-1-4525-4259-1 (sc)
ISBN:978-1-4525-4260-7 (hc)
ISBN:978-1-4525-4258-4 (e)

Balboa Press
A Division of Hay House
1663 Liberty Drive
Bloomington, IN 47403
www.balboapress.com
1-(877) 407-4847

Because of the dynamic nature of the Internet, any web addresses or links contained in
this book may have changed since publication and may no longer be valid. The views
expressed in this work are solely those of the author and do not necessarily reflect the
views of the publisher, and the publisher hereby disclaims any responsibility for them.

The author of this book does not dispense medical advice or prescribe the use of any
technique as a form of treatment for physical, emotional, or medical problems without the
advice of a physician, either directly or indirectly. The intent of the author is only to offer
information of a general nature to help you in your quest for emotional and spiritual well-
being. In the event you use any of the information in this book for yourself, which is your
constitutional right, the author and the publisher assume no responsibility for your actions.

Any people depicted in stock imagery provided by Thinkstock are models,
and such images are being used for illustrative purposes only.
Certain stock imagery © Thinkstock.

Library of Congress Control Number: 2011960699

Printed in the United States of America

Balboa Press rev. date: 12/01/2011

To my children.

This book explains who I am and who you are.
You both have the gift of inner wisdom.
Use it wisely.

With love,

Mom

Both heart and mind have to be involved in this journey towards liberation from the "self." The mind understands and concludes, connects and discerns, whereas the heart feels.

When our feelings become free of emotional reactions and dwell in love and compassion as their natural abode, our mind will be open to the great truths of universal significance. And the more we refer to these truths, the closer we will get to spiritual emancipation.

Ayya Khema, *Being Nobody, Going Nowhere:Meditations on the Buddhist Path*

Contents

Acknowledgments

Very special thanks from the center of my being to my dear guide, who has encouraged me to present all the lessons received in a book; to my husband for volunteering so much of his time and knowledge to make this possible and for keeping me on the right track; and to my children for always believing in me.

Special thanks are also due to all those wonderful beings who have contributed in many ways to make this possible: to Janet for recommending Balboa Press; to Maureen for reading and commenting on the draft of the book and stimulating me to go on; and to Anna, my dear daughter, for creating the beautiful book cover.

Furthermore, I want to thank all those various beings with whom I have crossed paths who in one way or another have guided me to where I am right now.

Disclaimer

The author and the publisher disclaim any liability arising directly or indirectly from the use of this book. The author is not a medical doctor or any other kind of medical practitioner and will not diagnose conditions, perform medical treatment, prescribe medications, or interfere with the treatment of a licensed medical professional. The author is not engaged in rendering medical services, and this book should not be construed as medical advice, nor should it take the place of regularly scheduled appointments with a health care professional. Spiritual counseling is not meant to replace conventional medicine but rather to complement and enhance it. It is recommended that you, the reader, see a licensed physician or licensed health care professional for any physical or psychological ailment you may have. *No warranty, express or implied, is delivered by the author or publisher with respect to the contents of this work.*

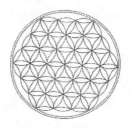

Introduction

A Letter to My Children

Dear Anna and Stephen,

I promised my guides I would write the book they so much insisted on. It has taken quite a long time for me to finally give in to their request and collect in this book the experiences and lessons received in this very special life of mine. Now you will understand why your mother was so *different* from other mothers and why she was often considered strange in her teenage years, as I could always see the truth that lies beyond the veil of reality. I want you to know and believe that life is a magical journey because many magical things that defy explanation have always happened in my life, as you have often witnessed. This is my legacy to you both, with the hope that you will never give up or forget this very important part of who you really are.

My dear ones, you do not need a master's or a PhD degree to write a book or write your own experiences in a journal. We are all one, and our experiences are as valid and as true as the next person's. You do not need a degree to validate them. There are many books that have been published under what is now called "New Age"—when I grew up the topic was called "metaphysics—by authors who have college degrees, and this is fine. But I do not want you think that because you do not have a master's or a PhD you cannot write about your own experiences and dreams. I guess the confirmation that you have a higher education provides credibility with the readers, and it implies that the writer has a profound knowledge of the subject and can provide valuable information that somehow has escaped everybody else. I want you to know that when you connect with your inner self, all the information that comes through is valid because you are all connected to the one "God," "Source," "Energy," etc. The words that you write in your journal pour out of this very special place within you and are unique to your own life.

I believe we should all write our own experiences in a personal journal and read them every day or periodically. This will help us to understand ourselves and be appreciative of life and others. This life we have been given is a special journey with very personal experiences. We all have a mission in our lives, but very often we stray from the path that we selected before coming into this reality, either by the will of others or because we do not dedicate any time to finding out who we really are. This is the most important lesson in our lives, a lesson that is not taught by family, school, or college. It is a lesson that unfolds through the experiences we live, but, in order to learn it and evaluate all the consequences, we need time to observe our lives or we will never be able to draw any conclusions.

My life has been, so far, a wonderful adventure. I have not always felt this way, but I have had tremendous help all these years. My guides have taken care of me with such patience and determination that I want to write this book to give thanks to all the wonderful guides who are accompanying me in this present journey. It has taken me many years of interpreting my dreams, of searching for answers, of reading about other people's experiences, of crying, and of conquering despair to get to where I am today. This has not been an easy journey, and I am still on the path to a destination that it is not within my reach yet, but I have been instructed to share my experiences with you (as well as others) so that you might recognize what is happening to you. Hopefully my experience, the knowledge I have accumulated in my life and that now I am passing on to you both, will help you to understand your own mission a bit better.

As you both know, I was born in Italy after World War II. My grandfather wanted a grandson and was not prepared to receive a granddaughter instead. I do not really remember if my father was happy with my arrival because when I arrived in a cold November night he was working in South America, where a large number of Italians had migrated after the war to find jobs. So my arrival was not what you would call a happy event.

My first years were spent with my mother and we lived with my grandparents in a small apartment in the military barracks where my grandfather was stationed. I have fond memories of those years because I love the city where I was born, with its rivers and surrounded by the beautiful Dolomite Mountains, always capped by snow and lined with green valleys. I still remember a picnic we had on a nice, warm summer day in one of these valleys and, even though I cannot remember the people who were there or the food we ate, I do remember the green that surrounded us that day. For the first time in my life, I felt in touch with nature and in my own little piece of heaven on earth.

I spent the first seven years of my life in relative comfort and surrounded by the love of my grandparents. I do not remember when my mother left me to join my father in South America. I did not even realize that the man who came to visit us a couple of times during those years was my father. To me, he was just a stranger, a friend of the family, and I did not feel for him the love I was supposed to feel.

During one of those visits, my parents decided it was time to take me with them to South America and I left my grandparents without knowing that I would never see my grandfather again, as he died of lung cancer two years later. A part of me went with him.

This is when my own personal journey starts: living in a new, strange country with two people who, even though they were my birth parents, I did not know that well, and without any relatives and friends. I can now say that thanks to this very special family situation, I withdrew within myself and discovered that the world outside was not the only one that was real. I was just eight when I realized that I was different from the other children, because my dreams would predict events that would happen to me and the people close to me, and to this day they have never failed me (as you know from personal experience). I also noticed that if I thought long enough about something, this something would happen. Somehow I was in tune with a part of me that was just as important as the physical one and was a participant in what happened in my life.

I could sense danger, feel the thoughts of the people around me, and look at their souls without them even knowing it. I will always be grateful to my parents for their acceptance of this gift of mine. They never tried to belittle it or make me feel bad because of it. They just accepted it and helped me any way they could in my quest to explore who I was. With this gift came the heavy responsibility of deciding on the best way to pass on the information I received through my dreams and feelings. How do you tell somebody you love that their death is near? There is no proven and accepted method to do so gently without instilling mortal fear in the person listening to this news. How do you tell your friends that you dreamed the face of your children months before they were born? How do you tell your friends that sometimes you must tell your son or daughter not to go out to a certain place because the feeling you have is negative and the message you receive is for them to stay home? How do you tell your friends that your whole life has been lived from the inside out and not from the outside in? Every decision I made and make is based on the dreams I receive because, if I don't follow the guidance provided and stray from the path that is shown to me. I know from experience nothing good will come of it. How do you tell your colleagues at work that you must go on to another job because you received the message to leave them behind and find another one? This method of living your life is not taught in any school or college and nothing prepares you for it. It is living by your inner guidance.

You should always pay attention to your dreams, always try to remember them. But as we all know as time passes, we tend to forget them. This is why you should keep a dream journal, your very own by your bedside, where you can jot down every dream that has impacted you and try to interpret it as impartially as possible. Try not to be emotional in your interpretation so that the information received is as clear as possible. And always date your writings. As you reread your dreams and interpretations, you will soon start noticing they are associated with events in your life or close to you. Mind you, not all dreams belong to this special category, but you will instinctively know which ones are the special ones, as they will be very vivid and you will invariably remember them when you wake up in the morning or soon after the dream has ended. These are the ones you need to record because they have been sent to you to guide and prepare you for a change that will certainly impact your life.

As the years go by, you will know that you are connected to something larger than yourself, and this something is sending you special messages to protect you and your loved ones and to prepare you in the best way possible for what is to come. Not all the messages that predict the future are set in stone. Some of them predict the future that you will have if you continue thinking the way you do, but if you want to change the final outcome then you must change your thoughts because nothing is set in stone. Some dreams are just what I call *brain chit-chat* and have no particular meaning, but the others are messages from the *inner world,* and you will always be able to tell the difference between them. The dreams from the inner world are very vivid and their symbolism is directly linked to animals or earth elements that have a meaning for you. They are also very scary because this is the only way to ensure that they will be embedded in your memory so you can remember them.

Please write them down in your dream journal. All of these dreams have a meaning and you need to take the time to work out the symbolism. It is like working out a word puzzle where the words are substituted by symbols, because symbols represent a much faster way to convey a message than the written word and the images the symbols represent are powerful enough to ensure that you will remember them when you wake up.

My dear ones, when the dreams I receive are linked to events in your lives, I will always let you know so you can be aware that a major lesson is about to happen and you can prepare for it. If you are aware that something is going to happen, then your awareness is heightened and the effects of the event to come are minimized or in some cases nullified.

You both have been blessed with special gifts. You both have prophetic dreams, see beings that are not in this physical dimension, and perceive feelings and energies around you that are invisible to the naked eye. Do not let these gifts go. Hold on to them as hard as you can because if you pay attention to them you will receive messages that will point you in the right direction and keep you safe. If you need an answer to an important question, think about it before going to bed and ask (aloud) for an answer, and it will surely come in one of your dreams or you will read an article or somebody you know or not know will provide you with the answer you seek.

You both know by now that we all have guides and angels who take care of and are linked to us for the duration of this life. These beings will never leave your side and I would suggest you talk to them daily if you can (even five minutes in your bedroom or while taking a shower) and ask for what you truly feel you want. By *truly*, I mean something that you believe can and will happen. Do not give up if the answer does not come right away. Keep on because it will come, but it may come in a way that you do not expect. This is the beauty of this life; your questions can be answered in so many different ways. Do not spend any time thinking how your prayers and questions should be answered, as our thoughts can be very limiting. But I can assure you that the answer best suited to you and your situation will come as if by magic.

Chapter 1

Live by Your Inner Guidance

Our bodies are not just physical. The physical body is the final product of all our thoughts, feelings, and images; however, we are much more than the physical we are so accustomed to seeing and taking as the only final reality. Our bodies extend way beyond the physical and this is why we are able to receive wonderful messages through our dreams when our physical bodies are asleep and our barriers are down. When we sleep, we are no longer aware of our surroundings, our defenses are down, and our ego is asleep. This is the time when communication with another level of consciousness that is part of us is possible. During the day we are bombarded by a barrage of news and information that does not allow for the connection to take place, and this is why it can only take place while we sleep when we have switched off our phones, iPods, TV, etc.

We all have the ability to dream and to remember our dreams. The symbols in our dreams are directly related to our experiences and fears. For example, I am afraid of water and tornadoes and these are the symbols that almost invariably appear in my dreams when they want to convey a message that I need to remember. I always remember these dreams because they are so vivid and the water is so frightening. Through the years, I have learned to interpret my dreams quite successfully and they have helped to steer my life in the right direction. You also have the choice to ignore them, but then be prepared to pay the price either with the loss of your job or an illness or other events in your life or that of your family that will influence your life forever. The dreams help you to prepare to face major events in your life with courage, faith, and peace.

This world is one dominated by fear. The news only conveys messages of fear. People only speak words of fear; they vibrate in fear and resonate in fear. Fear has become the major emotional vibration for billions of people.

Fear of losing your job; fear of losing your loved ones; fear of earthquakes, hurricanes, and tornadoes; fear of getting sick; of contracting an incurable disease; of losing your good looks; the recent fear of the recession; etc. The list could go on and on. Nobody speaks words of love, hope and faith, or anything positive.

This is why your dreams come to you using the symbolism of fear, because it is the one universal language we are all proficient in, but the message contained in them is always a message of courage, faith, and love. If you know what will happen then you will be better prepared to face the lesson to come. The only problem with dreams is that you will never be able to predict the time accurately. The events predicted could happen in a span ranging from a day to several years, but they will definitely happen.

Isn't it wonderful that we are not alone, that we are taken care of and loved? We are powerful beings, but the problem is that most of us are never aware of how powerful we are and struggle on in life alone without direction and hope, without knowing that there is a force that is part of us that is pure love. I have seen this force and I have felt the love, and nothing on this earth compares to it. The closest I have come to this type of love is the love I feel for my children. This is the force that compels most mothers to protect their children at all costs, even at the risk of their own lives; love does not rationalize, it just feels and is.

During a meditation many, many years ago in England, I saw a wonderful, translucent, pale-yellow light envelop me, and I felt a wave of love so powerful that I wanted to share it with all those around me. The love I felt was so overwhelming that all hates, fears, and problems were forgotten and transmuted instantaneously. This happened another time also years ago and, unfortunately, I have not been able to repeat this wonderful experience again. But while it lasted, I felt connected with and was part of the force we call "God" or "Source." This is why I firmly believe that all those who kill or injure others *in the name of God* are completely mistaken. There is no *my God versus your God* or *my God is better than your God* because there is only one God with different names, and this "God" is pure love, and pure love, by its own nature, transmutes hate, racism, and all the negative feelings that have been part of the human race since the beginning of time into love. Anything negative that comes into contact with this pure love cannot stay negative because it is transmuted into love on contact.

I could have remained in this feeling of pure love forever. I did not want to come back to my reality, but as I have chosen to be part of this earth I had to come back and hopefully as a better person. This experience influenced my life and I have tried to help those I have come across who needed help. Helping is not just giving money to charities so they can do their work; helping is also sharing yourself and your beliefs with others so they can see a different way of living life. By teaching by example, you offer people a different perspective of living life. You show them that there is a connection with an inner world that is part of us, if we only choose to live life from within and not only from the outside.

Unfortunately, this world is divided among those who live from within (priests, clergy, monks, imams, nuns, etc.) and those who live from outside (the rest of humanity). We have created a division between people, between them and us, and it should have never been this way. We are all one. We are all part of the same "God," "Source," however you want to call Him/ Her. There is no reason for hatred, racism, etc., because we are all one. The color of your skin and your religion has been determined for the most part by your parents and the region of the world you were born in. How can we have a Christian if a baby were to be born in a Muslim country by Muslim parents? Likewise, how could we have a Muslim or Buddhist if a baby were to be born in a Christian country from Christian parents? We all need to strive to live from within because it is who we are. What goes on within determines what our physical bodies will look like and the experiences we will live in this life. If you believe in hate, violence, etc. and all your thoughts are devoted to these feelings, then you will live experiences that you will hate or make you hate others. Your life will never change because you have selected how you want to live and what experiences you want to have. In order to change, you must first realize that the experiences you are living in your life are generated by your thoughts, that nobody else is responsible for your life but yourself, and that if you want a change in your life then you must change your thoughts and feelings. You need to recognize that your thoughts are not leading you to where you want to go and then you must change them so you can change the energy you vibrate at. Thoughts are not abstract; they are very real and have an influence on who you are and how you live. They also determine and are a deciding factor in the illnesses you will suffer.

Quite a few times in my life I have been at the receiving end of strange illnesses that have forced me to be hospitalized for almost a week at a time, but the doctors never could come up with a diagnosis, as I was healthy. Now after some thought and some work from the inside out, I can tell you what happened every single time and what was the determining cause of my hospitalization. I had all the symptoms of different ailments, but there was no external cause for them because the cause was on the inside. In my particular case, when some of the situations in my life got too much to bear emotionally, my body responded to my thoughts by creating the symptoms of an illness that would stop me dead in my tracks and would force me to take stock of the situation at hand and give me time to regain the balance I had lost. It is all a question of balance: emotional, physical, spiritual. This life is all about balancing all the aspects of your life and never forgetting the most important one: the *inner you*. This is the one that is the *real you* and *always in command*. This is why I have learned to meditate and take time to go inward. I no longer let outside events get the best of me. I simply do not listen to more than one newscast a day and select only those TV programs that are funny and nonviolent, because there is already enough suffering in the world. There is no need to watch it being re-enacted on TV as well. I have learned to find ways to distress myself and try to keep the best balance I can in my life.

It is very important for you to dedicate some of your daily thoughts to the inner world, to go inward and pay a visit to your *inner you*. This is who you really are and where all your power resides. The power does not come to you from your work, your bank account, your family, your hopes, your disappointments, your anger, or your despair, as these are all temporary and transient situations and feelings. The power comes to you from *within*. You see, both the outside and inside of you constitute the one beautiful being that is *you*. If you only concentrate on the outside (material/mind) or the inside (spiritual/soul), you will never be the complete being that you are intended to be, but you will only be half of who you are intended to be and will never be able to live up to your true potential.

This is why I worry when I see people spending so much time watching TV and playing electronic games, because even though these programs make you relax and provide you with fun in your life, there is no time left to dedicate to the *inner you*. I can almost see your faces when you read this part, but do not take it badly as it is not my intention to tell you off in anyway. I just want you to be able to achieve everything you want in this life, and the time spent watching TV and playing games is like sand in the wind: it will blow away and leave you with nothing in your hands. You must dedicate ten to twenty minutes every day to meditate and go inward; practice and practice until it becomes second nature to you. This exercise, which is equivalent to the regular prayer in all religions, will clear your thoughts and help you focus on what it is that you want to achieve in your lives. And most important of all, it will keep the connection with your *inner you* active so you can identify your mission. Most humans turn to prayer only during times of crisis in their lives, but once the crisis has passed they forget and get on with their lives (the equivalent of taking a pill for a headache). If you keep the connection with your *inner you* alive, then you will be able to avert the crisis because you will know how to steer your thoughts in the direction you want to go and you will feel the love that is around and in you, and this love will always keep you protected.

You need to develop this link to your *inner being* that is like an umbilical cord. This is the most important lesson I have learned to date. Once you do this, information will start flowing to you in what could appear to be a magical way. The most astonishing thing is that this information is full of wisdom, common sense, and logic, and it pertains to you and your mission in this life. Sometimes you may also receive general information or information that is applicable to someone you know, and it is entirely up to you to decide if you want to share the information received with the rest of the world or someone you know. This is a decision that only you can make.

Many years ago I dreamed about my mother's death two and a half years before it happened, but I decided not to tell her or my father anything and used the time to make her life as comfortable as possible and to be near her as often as I could. We were all fortunate enough to be there with her at the moment of her passing. Not long ago I received another message regarding the next person in our close circle who is due to pass on, and as before I decided to keep the secret and let time run its course. This knowledge of things to pass is one of the most difficult things for me to accept, but I also know that there is nothing I can do and should do. My guides are just helping me to prepare in advance for a situation that will cause me sorrow. Right now I am doing my best to encourage this person to enjoy life and do something that she always wanted to do. I can only hope to succeed.

In general, I dream only of events that will affect my life and the lives of the members of my immediate family, and sometimes friends. I seldom dream of events that do not have an impact on my life, whether directly or indirectly, which I think is wonderful as the burden of knowing too many things in advance would be too much to bear.

Fifteen years ago the beginning of menopause caused me to develop panic attacks so severe they changed my life and restricted my activities to the point of inactivity. For five years, I lived from panic attack to panic attack; the whole of my life revolved around them. They occupied all my thoughts and feelings. I was desperate to find a cure, but the only thing that the doctors could do was to prescribe pills to diminish their effects. They could not pinpoint the physical cause that would trigger them. This caused me the additional suffering of going through a severe depression because I could not see any point in living the way I was. Every time one happened, I thought I was having a heart attack as all my system went out of whack and there was nothing I could do but swallow a pill.

One day, by pure synchronicity, I found a little book where the author who had suffered from these attacks spoke of how meditation had helped him to mitigate their effect and finally to cure himself. This started another chapter in my already unusual life, as I was introduced to meditation as a way of attempting to alleviate my health issue without knowing that meditation would open a wonderful new door into the unknown and lead me to a path where nobody I knew at the time had gone before.

One of the many benefits of my meditations has been the ability to communicate with one of my guides who imparts information, not just as personal lessons for my own education and development but also for the good of my family, relatives, friends, and the world in general. All the information I receive is in the form of short lessons on a variety of subjects that include health, emotions, energy, vibrations, other worlds, universes, etc. This is the information, the lessons I want to pass on to you for your own benefit and those around you. This information is full of wisdom and it always amazes me when I read it. I usually do not remember what I write as I always write while in a meditative state, so I need to read what I have written and invariably feel very happy at having been given this special gift.

So from this point forward, I will write the lessons as I have received them and I will continue to do so until the moment I stop receiving them (which I hope will not happen until it is my turn to pass on), as these lessons have opened my eyes and horizons. I have learned to see this world of ours in a totally different way, as it is much vaster, more vibrant, and more beautiful than I ever imagined. We are certainly not limited to only being a *body*, as this body of ours is but an infinitesimal part of who we are. It is only a suit, a temporary dwelling that houses our soul. I do not understand why so many beings in this dimension dedicate all their time and attention to the physical part of their bodies. You certainly need to keep your body clean, fit, and in good health, but to think that there is nothing else aside from this body is unreal and untrue. We are wonderful beings and I will never cease to repeat it: we are wonderful beings and it is a pity that we limit ourselves to just the body portion of our being. The fault for this type of thinking is not really ours as we are taught from a very early age that this body is very important and everything else outside the physical world belongs to the realm of the spiritual, intended as *religious*, not of spirit. Our senses go far beyond the five senses we use daily. There are so many universes out there that we cannot possibly count them all, or comprehend their vastness just by using our human physical brain.

If there is only one thing you remember from this book, please remember to go *within you*, as *your best friend resides within*.

Now dear ones, I am ready to pass on the lessons I have received so far, in exactly the same language they were given to me. Please read them with an open mind and remember that my own ego was not involved in these writings. If you do not understand something, leave it and go on. I suggest you return to the lessons you do not understand later, and you will see how you will begin to understand their meaning.

The main responsibility I assumed when I came to this life was the one of the caretaker. I had to care of my mother and later my children, my family, as well as other beings that life put in my path. As a caretaker, one must have the humility to know there are things you do not understand and the courage to pursue the truth, wherever it leads you. And this is where it all has led me.

Chapter 2

My Guide Officially Introduces Himself

The lessons presented here are given as they were conveyed to me. They can be read sequentially, in any order desired, or as inspired.

Part 1: Who Are You?

Who are you?

I am your Master Guide. You have a group of four guides assigned to you at different times, but I am, so to speak, the one in charge of you and your progress in learning the lessons you set for yourself for this lifetime. We have been together before, but this is the first time you have consciously acknowledged my presence. You have come a long way in a short time. Yes, what Irene told you about being here to teach is true, and you should concentrate all your efforts to achieve that. You are here to teach by your example.

How can I teach? I do not even like to teach.

You will in time. You will. You will dedicate these coming years to learning, studying, and meditation. Then you will be ready to reach out and teach.

Should I write a book about my experiences?

Yes, you should. It would be most interesting to people.

How can I write when I do not like to write?

I will help you to do it, like we are doing right now.

Yes, but with this exercise I am not sure if it is you or me speaking? How do I know I am channeling and it is not just my imagination?

I am Knenesset, from the tribe of Elohim, on a planet in a galaxy far removed from earth. I have been in service for many years, and with many people, including you. I am very tall, with long silvery hair and grayish-silvery skin. Can you feel my presence?

Yes, I can feel a tingling in my forehead and in my body. Is that you?

Yes.

May I see you?

Not yet, but you will in time.

Is there anything else I need to know?

Not at this moment. Good bye for now. This is enough for our first encounter.

In love and peace, thank you.

Part 2: The Million-Dollar Dream

Quite a few years ago, I dreamed I was receiving a check for one million dollars. I was given a check by a person I did not know. The only thing I still remember very clearly is that the man who was handing me the check had a burgundy jacket. Money is not part of my current reality, which is why it has not yet entered my life in full.

We sent you the dream where you received a check for one million dollars to convey to you the message that this is a reality you can aspire to. This million is yours only when you are ready to receive it. To become ready, you have to change your way of thinking and feeling about money. By ignoring its energy, the problem will get bigger and bigger. This is one of the lessons you came to learn in this life. You must learn to let this energy into your life. It is an energy that is good for you, and the time has come to let it flow into your life.

How do I achieve this? I ask for your assistance in this.

Think of money as an energy that is part of your daily life, as love, curiosity, compassion, and generosity are. Money is just another aspect of the love energy. You have dedicated many lives to the service of others, to helping others in need. By helping others in need, the *need* feeling has stuck to you. You have come to believe that need is equal to lack of money. Do you understand this?

Money is a source of joy, peace, and generosity. Open up to this energy and let it come into your reality. Open up your heart and let it in. Think about this energy every second of every day; think on how good it feels to have lots of it at your disposal to do the things you consider right for you, your family, and others. Think that it can help you to live the life you want. You never wanted to work. All through these thirty years you never wanted to work. You were forced to work by your father, and then by your own beliefs. You believed that your husband could not provide for the family and if you worked, you were ensuring your freedom and independence from him, in case something wrong happened. Well, nothing has happened, so it is time to give up this belief, give up your job, and give up your need for a job. Do what you really want to do and what you really like. How do you envision your life?

I would like to stay at home and at the same time have the means to travel to conferences, seminars, and to travel to Italy and other countries I want to visit. I want to participate in meditation classes and meet people.

Knenesset, what else is there for me to do?

Start with changing your thoughts right this instance. Open up to the million dollars that is already yours, for that is going to be the base of your future endeavors. Do not think on how it will come into your reality; just think that it is already part of your present reality. Feel it.

Is there anything else I need to know on this subject?

Yes, you are that energy. That million dollars is you, and you are that. Think about this. Create the feelings; feel them and it will appear in your reality.

Thank you for the message. Do you have a meditation that I could do to help myself feel this reality and change my current thoughts?

Repeat: I give thanks for the million dollars that are now entering into my life, for the good of all, and in peace. I give thanks for this energy that is now part of me. I am open to receive it right now and I can feel that it is now part of me and it will be only a fraction of time before it is manifested into my reality. Thank you.

In love and peace, thank you.

Dare to Dream

Today I want to talk about you.

Dalende, dare to dream! Work on your dreams. They will become your reality. Reality is nothing more than dreams come true. Do you understand?

This is a world of dreams, the sum of all the dreams, either positive or negative, of each speck of energy in this dimension. That is why there is so much chaos in the world. Nobody centers anymore. A great majority of souls are off center, thus their creations are off center as well. The major lessons you came here to learn are preset, but the future is not. As you learn them, you change your future. It is your present that dictates your future. You create it with every instance of your present. You are creating your future now. As any good architect knows, you need a blueprint to build a house. You need a blueprint to build your reality. Work at drawing your blueprint now and your reality will change. Dare to dream! Dreams are not idle ideas. They are the bricks of the future you choose to live. Do so for the good of all mankind and without hurting anyone.

What is this slight pain I feel in my chest?

Do not worry; your etheric heart is waking up. It is starting to stir. Your physical heart is fine. I am offering you the freedom to dream your life as you feel deep inside you that your life should be. Do not listen to other people: your parents or anybody else. Look deep inside yourself and follow your intuition. Intuition is the link to the soul. It is your higher self speaking. In order to follow it, you need to keep the channels open and learn to listen. Do not be swayed by other people's opinions, just follow your intuition. That is the secret of your life. It is a part of you that needs to be acknowledged by the physical you. All your guides and your higher self use the intuition channel to communicate with you. Always be open to listen to your intuition because it will never fail you. Your guides and your higher self know the lessons you have selected for yourself and they will always guide you toward them. Your objective in this life is to learn your lessons and to feel oneness with the other specks here with you. As a baby trusts its parents, so you should always trust your intuition.

You are ready to start walking on the path. That is why Irene (my previous much-beloved guide) has left you alone. She knows you are ready and do not need her assistance anymore.

I am still confused about the path I am to follow.

As I told you yesterday, you are ready to teach. The way you will do it will be shown to you soon enough. Just pay attention to the signs. Do not look for another job, because to teach is your job. That is why you came here. Do not worry about finances, as I know you do, because everything will be provided for you. As I told you yesterday, there is a lot of money waiting to come into your reality. Your lesson now is to open up to this energy waiting to come into your life. As you would trust your parents if you asked them for a loan, so you should trust your higher self and source. This is your reality. This money waiting for you is your reality. Just recognize it and trust it to become materialized. Enough for today.

In love and peace.

Creation and Manifestation

Good morning, Knenesset. I want to thank you for being here to talk to me. How do our thoughts work?

Sometimes they are not thoughts. They are only words said in the silence of your mind, a string of words with no consequences. In order for words to be effective, they have to be said aloud because then they become energy in movement. So if you want something in your life, say it out loud. It is no good just thinking about it. Thinking has no feeling (emotion). It is a linear string of words connected together with no feelings. Feelings are expressed only through the spoken word.

Images are better transmitters of energy. The mind works with pictures because it is the way it creates everything. Matter is manifested through images. People should use images to create what they want. In a way, it is very similar to the way an artist creates on canvas a picture of what he sees as his reality. When you paint a picture, you pay attention to the details, the color; you must fill in all the details that make up your picture of something. With silent words, that is impossible. Remember silent words carry no feelings and thus they do not create anything. They cannot create because they are devoid of the prime substance of feeling. If you want to create, speak aloud and feel the words. Create your images and feel them as you finalize your canvas.

Energy needs movement in order to rearrange creation to bring about manifestation. Everything is energy vibrating at different frequencies. Energy vibrates but does not move. To allow manifestation, it needs movement, and feeling is what moves the energy. You have to learn how to use this energy before you can manifest anything. Everything emanates a vibration generated by its energy. Learn to recognize these vibrations. Learn to feel this energy and you will become aware of images on this plane that you have never seen before. You will also see images of things from other planes that you have never seen before.

Everything is energy (including what appears to be void) that has a distinct vibrational pattern. All forms have their own specific vibrational pattern, which is what makes them unique in their essence. In order to create other forms, you need to change the vibrational patterns of existing matter, and you do this with feelings. Feelings rearrange the original vibrations of energy and create other forms. This is why *love* can heal/cure and change everything. Its vibrations are high because the feeling connected to it is so powerful and compassionate that transforms everything instantly. Whatever is done for the good of all creation is automatically for your own good as well, since we are all one, we are all sparks from the same Source. When we injure another form of creation, we also injure ourselves because we are one and the one cannot be separate in its oneness. So feel your dreams, do not think about them in silence, but feel them, picture them and fill them with feelings, and they will manifest because this is the law. Imprint this energy in your image, then give it feeling and it will exist.

In love and peace, thank you.

Money and Debt Mentality

I would like to talk about money again.

Why are you so obsessed with money?

Because I always had to do without and I have been in debt for years and would like to get out of the debt mentality. Can you help me and guide me to the solution of this issue?

You have to change your mentality and learn that comforts and the freedom to do what you want, when you want, does not come from money. It comes from the proper use of creative energy. You are making the mistake of confusing money with creative energy. Money is just one aspect of creative energy, but there are many other aspects of it. Money will not get you peace of mind.

You have lived all your life believing that money could come only from outside sources, that you could not generate this creative force by yourself, and, by thinking like this, you have created a dependency similar to a dependency on drugs, cigarettes, and alcohol. You are dependent on money coming from other people. You have to change this idea and see yourself as the center of your creative energy. *You can create money yourself or you can create circumstances and projects that will generate the money you want. You are the center of it.*

Repeat this to yourself every minute of every day: *I am the center of my creation and I can create anything I desire.*

You have empowered other people with the task of giving you money, but you have to empower yourself with this. *You hold the power* to create money for you; nobody else does. Also, you need to love money, show it your love. Do not just spend and use it without talking to it and thanking this wonderful manifestation of energy into your life. Thank every bill that comes into your life, and thank every bill that exits your life for the wonderful service it has provided to you.

If you want something to grow—a plant, a child, an animal, anything in creation—what do you have to do? You have to love them, don't' you?

Yes.

Well, it is no different with energy. Energy just waits for your love to create what you so lovingly desire. Examine your relationship to and feelings about money until now. You have ignored it. You have spent it continuously, and you have limited its coming (manifestation) into your life. Jobs are not the only source of income. Income can come in many forms and in many ways. Do not limit yourself to only one source. Change your views because they only perpetuate your limitations.

Now that you are finally getting out of debt, be aware of this wonderful energy that comes into your life in the form of food, clothes, and all the other things you need. You are just exchanging one form of energy for another. And be thankful, always thankful, for its presence in your life. Become aware of the presence of this wonderful energy, love it, and feel at ease with its use. Do not ignore it … or misuse it because then nothing will change.

Now on the million-dollar dream that you all sent me years ago, what is its meaning?

It means that it can come into your life only when you are ready to receive it, because until now you were not ready to receive it. You have resisted receiving things, including money, all your life. This will be our gift to you, but you have to prepare yourself to receive it. There is nothing wrong in receiving things. Be happy for it.

Why do I find it so hard to receive?

Because by not asking for things, you thought that the people around you (your family) would not notice you and love you more if you were accommodating and quiet.

Since your parents were never good at finances, you felt that you could not ask what there was not enough to go around, and you felt guilty for their lack … as if it was somehow your fault they had beliefs of lack. But learn to ask and love to receive and keep your money, lovingly. Do not squander it because you will only be offending nature by squandering its resources. Ask, receive, and use it wisely, and always with love and awareness. This creative energy is ready to work with you as soon as you ask. It has been waiting for your realization for a long time. But now, I think you are ready. Remember what I told you? Be always loving and respectful of Source's energy. Do not waste it.

The more you continued to ignore it, the more debt came into your life, until debt reached a point that forced you to focus on the problem. But you focused in the wrong way, because instead of seeing it as a call from Source to focus on your creative powers, you saw it as something to hide and keep out of your daily realization, to keep it in the background so to speak. You let it fester up to a point where, in the end, you were forced to look at it and do something to resolve the situation.

This is the first step in the process of changing your mentality regarding this issue. You are a creative person, and, as part of Source, can create all you intend to have in your life. The only limitations are the ones you impose on yourself. Look upon creation as a white canvas where you will draw a picture of everything you desire without limitations of any type.

You tripped over the same stone (debt) on the same path for years, simply because you turned a blind eye to it. You knew it was there, but you tried very hard to ignore its presence until this stone became a boulder so large that to continue on the path you had to acknowledge its presence and find a way around it without hurting yourself in the process. Now you can continue on the path because you have acknowledged its presence, focused on it, and found a way around it. You will see that from now on the path will be without stones, and creative ideas will flow naturally to you.

Keep up with your meditation; do not let it slip to the backburner. It is your link to us and Source and needs to be kept flowing. I am always with you (as the stone on your path), but I cannot communicate with you until you realize my presence and feel my energy. This should be a daily practice.

In love and peace, thank you.

Meditation on Manifestation

Picture a blank screen filled with matter/energy. This energy is just waiting for you to give it shape and direction. You have to use your thoughts, intent, and desire (emotion) to give it shape. Remember to clear any existing conditions that might be limiting you because these conditions will keep on limiting you until they are cleared. Once the clearing has taken place, then you will be ready to go to your blank screen and work on the energy/matter there. For this, you need extremely clear ideas, and this will take some work. You, and most people, tend to go back and forth between different ideas. Just take one, only one, stick to it, and see what happens. Keep it in your mind for the time necessary for it to appear in this reality. Remember to create only one thing at a time. Concentrate only on one thing at a time. Do not think of other things, because this will only confuse the picture, dissipate your energy, and there will be no manifestation.

Make this your project. Think about one component at a time and see it through until it is finally manifested. Slow down your thoughts and see what you really want manifested first. Give it some thought until you have a clear idea of what you want to manifest in your reality. Always remember to mention that it should be manifested by divine grace, for your highest good and the good of all, and give thanks for its manifestation.

Start now with a new project (idea) and see what happens, but stick to it until it is manifested. Do not give up before manifestation happens and do not change ideas halfway through the process because nothing will happen as the energy will lose direction and intensity. This is the basic procedure for manifesting. I hope it serves you well.

In love and peace, thank you.

Energy and Matter

Does energy convert into matter?

Yes, matter is a form of energy that is given its physical form by thought. That is why you can change any matter through thought at any given time (now for example). Nothing is static or fixed. Everything moves, changes, because everything responds to thought forms. Bodies emit electrical impulses because their basic matter is energy. Watch your thoughts because they will manifest. You should know this better than most since you always manifested everything you thought with emotion (usually fear), including illnesses. What you have to do now is empower yourself with positive thoughts of how you want your life to be according to the mission you chose for this lifetime. That is why you need to meditate and keep in touch with your higher self. This will keep you on the path to your highest good. Watch every single thought because when it persists over a period of time it will manifest whether you want it or not, and not exactly for your highest good. Start working on this *now.*

Why is fear such a powerful emotion that manifests almost immediately? Because you and many other beings believe in it; because through time you all have been led to live in a world based on fear. Look around. Don't you feel the fear surrounding you? Almost everybody on this plane fears something: the loss of health, loss of homes, loss of jobs, loss of families, loss, loss, loss … Everything represents some form of loss. Nobody thinks out of joy, out of believing that he/she is entitled to all the good things life has to offer. Your life will be what you believe it to be.

Always remember that you are not you. You are the manifested thought of your higher self. Remember that this plane is nothing but a hologram, and, as such, *you can change it at any time.* That is why it is so important to keep in touch with your inner self. This is written in all religions. They all require prayer at least twice a day because it is the only way you can communicate with your inner self, so follow the path that you have set for yourself in this lifetime. Idle thoughts only generate confusion … Don't you see the confusion around you? People are confused. They do not know what to think and do anymore. They look like lost sheep; be the *master of your thoughts* and you will be the *master of your life*.

Remember that fear is a powerful tool used by a few to control the great majority. It is through the use and spreading of fear that they make their livelihood. It is through fear that they sell their ideas and products. They keep you in bondage for all of your lifetime on this plane. If you only knew how truly magnificent and powerful beings you are … You do not need fear; you do not need to believe in any of the dark messages out there. You only need to believe in *yourself* and keep in touch with your higher self. When you are one with your higher self, you can create anything you desire, always for your own good and that of your brothers and sisters. When you are separate from your higher self, then you can only create chaos and confusion because you are not working for your highest good. If you are one with your higher self and follow your inner voice, then nothing can stop you and fear will be no more. Always remain in love, and work from love, and everything will be fine. Love yourself, love Mother Earth, love this life of yours, and love the lessons (trials and tribulations) you have selected for yourself to live. Love everything and everybody around you because you all are truly magnificent.

In love and peace, thank you.

Your Whole Being (Who You Really Are)

Today, we are going talk about the *being*, not just the human being but the whole being. You all live in several dimensions at the same time, even though your major awareness is centered in this dimension, the third one. You are experiencing things that are happening in different dimensions at the same time and all those flashes of intuition, premonitions, déjà vu, and gut feelings in general are nothing more than the experience of the life you are presently living in all these dimensions. Why are gut feelings called gut feelings and not brain feelings? Because the connection to all your other bodies is through your solar plexus chakra, which is located in the solar plexus area. All the information that is not processed by your five physical (three-dimensional) senses comes through this chakra. It is in a sense a sixth sense, but not in the context of a supernatural sense. It is just as natural as the five you are familiar with and it is the sense that is used to transmit to you the information that is gathered in the other dimensions. When you like or dislike another being, without even knowing him/her personally, it is simply because you sense their energy field. If their energy vibrates at the same frequency as yours, then you will certainly

17

like this person, but if their energy is inharmonious with yours, then you will not like this person. Everything is energy, as I have already told you. All relationships are just an exchange of energies between two sources. Energies between sources can be harmonious or dissonant. But, even if they are dissonant, you can always change the situation by neutralizing this dissonance by applying its opposite and then start from there.

Remember everything is energy, and everything is nothing more than an exchange of energy. All thoughts, all experiences, are just exchanges and emissions of energy. Once you learn this, then everything becomes easier. Nothing is purely physical in this dense plane. Everything is just a hologram generated by your higher being who is trying to experience the complexities of living in such a dense environment. Why is it so dense? Because the density is needed to prevent you from instantaneously creating effects that would cause damage to the rest of creation.

If you could manifest your thoughts instantly, there would be a lot of chaos, since you have not yet learned to control your thoughts. Density is placed here to help you to learn to control your thoughts and actions, to give you time to learn how to manifest for your own highest good and that of others. The events in your dimension are nothing more than your thoughts manifested, and you can all see the chaos and destruction that is around you. Can you imagine if this dimension were not as dense as it is what your thoughts would do to the rest of Creation? You would end up destroying everything.

Look at the earth, the sky, and the beauty around you. It is so diverse and so perfect. Everything in nature happens for a reason and within a structured, perfect, pre-established, and well-thought-out pattern. It is the reflection of the thought of Source; it is his creation. We are his creation as well, but we have been given free will. In other words, we are free to do and think what we want, when we want. We are responsible for our own thoughts and actions. Our mistake lies in thinking that this dimension is all there is in our lives. It is not so. We are multidimensional beings, living one life at a time in several dimensions at the same time. But our awareness is only centered on this earth life, because this dimension is so dense, vivid, and real to us that we forget who we really are. This dimension is nothing more than a school where we come to experiment and learn to think in a way that is constructive, not only for ourselves but for the rest of the sentient beings sharing this lifetime with us. This is why manifestation is not instantaneous; there is a safety valve that has been built into this dimension.

Let's say somebody does something that upsets you so much that you wish he or she was dead. How would you react if this person would immediately die in front of your eyes? And this is just one example. How many times haven't we said, "I wish he (or she) was dead or just disappeared from my life?" We are here to learn to master our thoughts, to learn to live in the *now*, to learn that it is with every *now* that we build our future, that the objective of a life on this earth plane is to learn the lessons that we will carry with us for the rest of our lifetimes, that we are now the result of many lessons learned in the sum of all our lives.

We are wonderful beings with a tremendous capacity for love, because love is the main ingredient of all creation. People often speak of tragedies with fear or sadness, but we should thank the beings who set themselves up to be participants in these tragedies for the tremendous lessons on compassion and love they teach us. If you spare a minute and think about this, you will see that tragedies bring people together. They cancel hate, racism, and fear. They bring out the best in every person involved in this play. By the best, I mean love, compassion, caring, sharing, etc. So tragedies are necessary teaching tools, because they teach us the lesson of love, pure love, without any limitations. Unfortunately, many sentient beings take a long time to learn their lessons, because they become too involved in the density of this plane. They get caught in the mesh, so to speak, of this reality. They should learn to listen to their inner voice, because we all have it, but, to do this, they have to learn to quiet their exterior surroundings and go within. It is only when you learn to go within that you will hear it. Always pay attention to this voice/feeling, because it will show you the path to your highest good. But if you do not make the time to go within, then you will wander on this plane as a lost sheep not knowing what to do or where to go, scared of your surroundings. In other words, you will wander through this life lost and in fear.

In love and peace, thank you.

Remote Viewing

I was doing some research on remote viewing, a subject that interests me quite a lot, as well as everything that deals with energy fields.

Why are you interested in remote viewing?

Because of the possibilities of its application. They are infinite.

Remote viewing is nothing more than meditation. When you meditate you are actually practicing remote viewing. In your particular case, you have not yet found the black screen all remote viewing books refer to, because you are meditating only for the pleasure of it and to balance your energies. Your meditations still do not have a specific objective. Once you define your objectives, then you will practice remote viewing.

Do not buy any of the tapes that companies are selling on remote viewing, because you are already there. They will not teach you anything new. You just have to focus your meditation on a specific objective and then you are there. Remember that if you purchase a tape that teaches you how to use your mind, the same tape could also contain subliminal commands to control your mind. Stay away from them and anything that has to do with mind control. I will tell you how to do remote viewing.

The famous black window that remote viewers talk about is nothing more than the link to the universal mind. It is a place where there is no time, space, or dimensions. It is all there is. Once you reach that window or door, you enter *mind* and as part of it you can see whatever it is you want to see. It is like one part of yourself looking at all of you. That is all there is to it. It is just practice and focused meditation and nothing more. Do not let anybody tell you anything different.

The governments using it now cannot call it meditation because that would have a religious connotation, and so they have named it remote viewing. There is a lot of meditation being practiced right now for mind-control purposes. If you want to do a remote viewing meditation, you only have to enter your meditation, and, once in a meditative state, establish an objective you want to reach or a place you want to visit. Images will start appearing on your black screen. Do not manipulate any of these images and do not try to interpret them with your physical senses, because then you will not get the real meaning of it. Just be an observer; observe without judging or interpreting. Let the image develop and once it is over and you come out of your meditation then write everything you saw and felt. Only then you will be able to interpret correctly everything you saw. This technique can be applied to anything you want to see—a place, a person, situations in your life—and it must be done consciously.

We have sent you messages in your dreams because that was the only time we could communicate with you. Now your intuition is better and the dreams will diminish because you are open to receive the messages directly without going through the dreaming process. Your life is changing; you have come to realize that. Your view of life is changing, and a whole new universe is opening in front of you. You can do remote viewing now if you want because you are ready for it. Select a target idea and experiment with it. Remote viewing is a very complex and dangerous subject. Up to now, it has only been used to control other people and to control situations, but it has wonderful applications. You can influence your environment for the better. You can set the scenario for wonderful things to happen. Remember that the black screen is nothing more than the window to the universal mind, and it is not empty; it is full of substance waiting to be molded and shaped and projected into reality.

So go ahead; you are ready for it. Do it on your own, under our guidance, which is really the best way to proceed. Actually it is the only way to proceed. Everybody should practice remote viewing under the vigil eye of their guides and following the intuition of their higher self. Practice it and, when you do, be reassured that I will be with you.

In love and peace, thank you.

We Are Multidimensional Beings

I find that I am living more and more outside this earth reality and I do not understand fully what is happening to me. Yesterday I went for a walk, and, even though I was doing something physical like walking, I felt as if I was sliding through time and my surroundings were far away and not part of me. Why is this happening so much lately?

That is because you are starting to realize that we all live in different dimensions at the same time. You are not entirely here and you are not entirely in the other dimensions. You are everywhere. You are part of everything there is. Now it is more evident in your life, because you have realized it.

So is this normal?

Yes, it is. And it will get more pronounced, so much so that you will start seeing things and beings that are not physical. You will start to deal with these energies and feel them as you do now when you meditate. Always keep an open mind when you channel, like right now, because sometimes ego does not know how to interpret the information you receive but needs to interpret what you receive (to make sense of it on its own terms) and sometimes that interpretation is wrong. So always keep an open mind. Do not interpret what you receive, just write it down and give up your ego's need to analyze everything.

You are expanding your perceptions. That is why it seems to you that you are not all here, because in reality you are not. Your perception is encompassing other dimensions of reality, and when that happens the physical tends to blur and fade in the background. You see, you are not physical beings at the exclusion of everything else; you are also, and for the most part, spiritual beings. This earth dimension is only one of many, many dimensions, but it is one of the densest dimensions. Density is so thick here that everything appears solid when in reality they are not. Objects are only a conglomerate of particles held together by thought energy. They are held together so tightly that they appear solid, but in reality they are not. The appearance of solidity is only a perception of your physical brain. The brain can only process information received through the five senses. The mind perceives differently, because the mind is not bound by this physical environment and it is part of the whole.

The reason for you to be here is to unite the physical with the spiritual, to become whole again. You do not realize the physical until you are aware of the spiritual and vice versa. The lessons that will make you a whole spiritual being are only learned in the physical dimension, because it is only here that we experience division-separation. It is only here that we become aware of the different portions that are part of us. You cannot be all physical, as you cannot be all spiritual in this dimension, because then you would be off center. The physical gives you the tools to live on earth and the mind gives you the insight to live the lessons you chose before you reincarnated. If you were all physical, then you would not know what you came here to do and you would feel disconnected from your true self. If you were all spiritual, you would feel totally disconnected from your surroundings and your life in this physical plane would have no meaning. The physical and the spiritual sides of yourself have to work in unison through this life-experience if you are to achieve what you came here to learn and do. Feel the connection between your two selves and keep this connection open and flowing at all times. Only by doing this you will live a life of balance and service to others.

At this moment, you are starting to live with the spiritual side of yourself. You are learning to walk in a balanced way, and every learning process takes effort and commitment. But once you learn to live this way, there is no turning back, because you become a whole being and your two halves cannot live without each other. They learn to share information, to trust each other, and to love each other. Once you become whole, there is no division possible, because if you consciously try to separate again you will immediately know that you are not whole and you will experience a feeling of lack, of missing something essential in your being.

Reversing Your Energy Flow

On another subject, for the money energy to flow into your life, you have to reverse the energy flow you have used for so long.

Reverse it? How do I do that?

You are on the right path. You have paid your debts almost, and, once you have done that, you will have reached the zero point zone, because you will have stopped the depletion of energy and there will be no more energy going out. Once you have reached this point, you can start building up your energy again in a positive way, seeing it coming in and being exchanged for other energy. So the full circle of flow will be reestablished. There will be energy coming in and going out in a normal cycle, not just going out and very little coming in as before when you created such an imbalance in that aspect of your life.

Remember everything is energy and you have to learn to deal with these energies according to their true nature. Money, paper money, is nothing in itself. It is just a symbol for energy; it represents energy. By the way, this is one of the lessons you set yourself up to learn in this life. In most of your past lives you were without money, because either you did not need it because of you being of service to others (as in Tibet, India, Spain, etc.) or you did not have enough confidence in yourself to bring this energy into your reality (as in France, Italy, etc.). You decided to use this lifetime to finally change these series of experiences that have been going on for so many of your lifetimes. You have learned many lessons so far and you are now learning one more. Money is not a living being in itself. Money is only a reflection of the energies that manifest it and keep it in this reality. Money is not a monster or a devil; money is not a god to be worshipped. Money is just energy—a manifestation of energy, like everything else surrounding you. It is just a form of energy, but you already know that. Now comes the fun part: using and directing this energy to do what you desire to do. You cannot create money because it is energy that is already here, so there is no creation involved. You can only give it purpose, set up your holographic picture as clearly as you can, and give it intensity until creation it is manifested. This trinity is nothing more than a formula for manifestation on this plane. Dalende, you are now bringing together in this lifetime your physical and spiritual sides, as they have been separate in your previous lives. You were either physical or spiritual. Now the time has come for you to be one.

The things around you in this dimension have been created by all the other sentient beings that have reincarnated here. Everything manifested in this dimension is somebody's creation. You create all the time, either bad or good. Fear is the greatest creator in this plane, and when fear is the primary ingredient of a creation nothing good comes out of it. You have to understand that nothing created by other beings will be part of your reality unless you are tuned in to their thoughts, their wavelengths. Nothing can really affect you unless you share the same reality. In other words, why do you look more like your mother than your father? Simply because you are tuned into her reality and not your father's. If you change your reality to reflect somebody totally different, in time you will change until you will look as the image you have chosen as your new reality. Do you understand?

This is why, during the great depression in the United States (which was nothing more than a reality shared—through fear—by the majority of its beings), some people were not affected and had a good life because the depression and the fear that it caused were never part of their individual realities. *You create your own reality out of fear or love or passion. We are all creators.*

You can create wonderful things as well as horrible ones. People create what they believe in, usually out of fear, and in thus doing they set themselves up for some very hard lessons. Do you understand the existence of different dimensions now? Do you see how many realities exist in this dimension alone? No two people have or share the exact same reality. They might share similar realities but not exactly the same one, because each reality is unique to its creator. So on earth alone you have billions of realities coexisting and interacting with each other. And you thought there was only one!

This is why each one of you should follow your own heart and mind, so that you can live your own personal reality, your own personal lesson, the one you selected before reincarnation. This does not mean to be insensitive to what and who is around you. Treat them as you would like them to treat you: with love and respect, always with love, respect, and compassion. You are all equal. You all come from the same Source. Nobody is better or more powerful than anybody else. How could you be? You are all made of the same substance and are part of the same One. How could one part be better, more powerful, or more important than the other? This is reflected in your bodies. Is your heart more important than your liver? Is your liver more important than your kidneys? The unity of these organs makes up your body, and by working together they ensure the well-being of your body. If one fails, the others suffer, and you might even die. If your heart fails, you are dead. If your liver fails, you are dead. If your kidneys fail, you are dead. Do you see what I mean? How can you determine which one is more important? Another consideration is that when organs fail they sure make your reality miserable.

As your consciousness expands vertically and horizontally and all around you, you will become aware of other dimensions. There are as many dimensions as there are realities. Even in the fourth or fifth dimensions, that are the ones following yours, there are infinite realities creating infinite perceptions of the same dimension, and thus in a way creating infinite dimensions. Do you understand this concept?

Yes, I think I do. Thank you.

Create your reality; the one you came here to experience. Follow your heart and your mind; do not let yourself be taken in by fear, the fear created by other sentient beings. Some very powerful changes will happen on earth in the years to come, but they will affect you only in the measure of your reality. If you believe in and are afraid of hurricanes, fire, tornadoes, or earthquakes, they will surely be part of your reality, but if you don't, they will not. They will slide by you without touching you.

Always remember this: *You will experience what you believe in and what you are afraid of. You will experience whatever your reality is. Fear is a powerful emotion as much as love is. Sentient beings have had eons to practice the use of fear and are attracted to it by the strength of its emotion. Fear creates emotion and emotion creates fear. They are linked. Love is also a strong emotion, but much less practiced.*

In love and peace, thank you.

The Use of Energy

Today, let's talk about energy. Everybody should learn how to use energy and become familiar with all aspects of energy. Since we are energy, it only makes sense that we should do so.

Personally, I do not know much about energy, aside from its regular uses in heating, transportation, etc. I do not know how to use this type of subtle energy that we are composed of. I can feel it, but I still do not go beyond feeling it. Now I can locate and feel you around me. What else do I need to know?

You need to know how to use it in your daily life.

I can see that this is going to be a difficult lesson.

No, not necessarily. Expand your mind. Do not let your ego get in the way and try to interpret what I am going to say. Just keep your mind open and keep the channel open, which is all you have to do. No interpretations from your ego.

Everything around you is energy and as such it vibrates at different rates. If you vibrate at the same rate, you will attract others with the same vibration, if you don't, you will just repel them. The trick is to find out the vibrational level of the things surrounding you. Once you find it out, then you can vibrate at the same rate to attract it or vibrate at a different level to repel it. Easy.

Well, this is easier said than done. How do I find out the rate of vibration of people or objects surrounding me?

You will find it out by looking at them with your third eye, not your physical eyes. Your third eye is in place to do just this, to identify the vibrations around you. And if your mind (through your intuition) agrees that you should bring this person or object into your sphere, then you should replicate the same energy vibrations. If your intuition tells you not to do it, then just let it go and you will automatically repel each other.

So what you are saying is that we need to activate and use our third eye?

Yes.

How do I do that?

Well, yours is already active, you just need to exercise it a bit more with specific meditation exercises for the third eye.

As?

When you meditate, focus on your third eye chakra. Feel its energy vibrating and imagine an eye opening in front of you, looking at you.

I have already seen it, sometimes, during my meditations.

Yes, I know. You need to practice more. When your eye opens, you can look through it and see things you have never seen before. You can also start to feel the energies around you. You have many more senses than the five physical senses. They are all part of you, but you have to learn to use them daily as you do with the others. Your intuition and your third eye are just two more of your nonphysical senses.

As an exercise, feel the vibrations of the objects surrounding you. Do not touch them because, if you do, you will be using your physical senses. Get close to the objects and feel them vibrate, feel their energy. Some vibrate at very slow rate. Always feel the space around you for unknown energies. You share your living space with many other forms that are not visible to your physical eyes, but they are there. If you stretch your arms and close your eyes, you can feel them. These forms can communicate with you, but only after you acknowledge their presence. It is always a matter of free will. Only by exercising your free will you can communicate. Get a one-dollar bill and feel its energy. What do you feel?

It is a warm feeling. I cannot feel any particular energy, which must mean that it has a low rate of vibration, but I can feel a slight warm feeling when I pass my hand over it.

That is the energy of money. Each person and object has its own particular energy signature like your fingerprints. They are specific to that object or person.

Many centuries ago, people were able to recognize these energies, and their vision of this dimension was completely different from yours. That is why you had tales of miracles, visions, dragons, and winged beings, because they could see what man's physical eyes could not and could hear what ears could not. As I told you yesterday, there are many realities, but you have to open up to them.

Well, I know about hearing, because somebody shouted in my ear a few times in the past.

Work at being aware during every moment of your daily life of everything surrounding you. Learn to feel the energies surrounding you. Learn to listen to them whispering in your ears. Listen to your intuition; expand your physical horizon.

Yesterday you taught me how to create the things I feel are right for my life at this moment: identify what I want, picture it clearly in my mind, and focus consciously on it until manifestation happens. Now I have a dilemma. I want to create money (dollar bills) to use to purchase travel tickets, computers, a car, a house, etc. I am confused because I do not know if I have to picture the bills or the things I want to create.

It is real easy. Create the bills that you see yourself using to pay for the objects you want. Actually imprint the energy around you with your clear thoughts of what type of bills you want, and then see yourself using this infinite supply of bills paying for the objects you want. Start now. Take something that you really want to create and do it now. It will work, you'll see.

Always remember that it should be for the good of all concerned, because for the mind there is no good or evil. You can create bills to do good things or bad things. You are the creator of what you want. You have the free will to do what you want. Energy is just energy. You are the one who will determine if the energy will be used for good or bad deeds. Those are conditions that are typical of this dimension. Evil is the counterpart of good and vice versa. When you start this experiment, cover all the angles, including that it should be for the good of all concerned, because then the mind will have a very clear blueprint and definite instructions on what you want to create.

When you create, you have to act as the creator and think of all the details, consequences, and interactions that your creations will have and cause. You are not creating something in a vacuum that is separate from its surroundings. You are creating something that is linked to already existing things in your world. Your creation should not cause disruption or harm anybody, or anything else. It should be a creation in harmony with its surroundings. Always remember this: create only harmonious and loving (through love) things.

Well, this brings to an end your mini lesson on creation. Now test it and see what happens.

In love and peace, thank you.

Nothing Will Change if We Do Not Take Responsibility for Our Lives

It is a major burden to find out that we are responsible for our lives and all our actions. Maybe I should not call it a burden, but an *enlightening experience.*

To assume total control and responsibility for all our thoughts and actions in this lifetime is very empowering. We are part of Source and as such we have the ability to create *what we want to experience* in this life and *how we want* to experience it. We decide on what we want (our soul mission in this lifetime) before we reincarnate. The *how* portion comes during this life. The *what* is fixed, but the *how* is the variable in this equation.

Most of us get distracted by this dense dimension and lose track of how we want to accomplish the mission we set up for ourselves. Absolutely everything that happens to us in this dimension is created by us, by our thoughts, beliefs, and fears. Nothing much is being created at the moment through love, which is the real essence of this dimension. This is the dimension of love, not fear. That is why everything on this earth is so chaotic and confused.

Dear ones, you are working from the opposite end of the same spectrum without even knowing it. You are using a completely different energy level (fear) from the one you are supposed to use (love). The few people who are in positions of power (human power that is) use fear as their control tool. Nothing controls other beings more than fear. Fear is strong and creates strong emotions. These emotions are the basic ingredient for manifesting what you most fear. Love is a much gentler and more stable emotion; there are no ups and downs. When love comes from the heart, love is an energy that can mend absolutely every human condition on this plane, but love does not provide the highs and lows that fear does. Love is a more subtle, level energy. Fear has more peaks and is comparable to a drug addiction. It shoots adrenaline through your physical body, it upsets your stomach, and it makes your heart beat faster. Strong fear paralyzes you. It makes your physical body respond in a physical way. Love does not. When you feel this Source love, you do not have the same physical responses in your body. You just feel this great all-encompassing warmth that lights and changes everything. As a gentle wave washing to shore readjusts the sand, so does love. Love changes the landscape with its warmth and gentleness. Once you experience this type of Source love, it stays with you and everything else, including fear, just fades in the distance.

Some human beings use fear because it produces money for them. They have become salesmen of fear and their sales are skyrocketing. Not a day goes by on earth without a new fear being sent out into the market, so to speak. As soon as a fear is unleashed, then a control method for that fear is also sent out. So if you want to avoid what this fear does to you, you will have to buy whatever it is that will cure you, or at least put this fear on hold for a while.

Do you understand the mechanics of this? It is very simple really. Fear has become a commercial product that brings in very high revenues, quite sadly. Love cannot be marketed in the same way, because love does not bring in the same revenue. Who will buy love? When you come from love, your perspective changes; fear does not have control over you. *Love heals, fear makes you ill—it is a poison*—because your true self (which includes your physical body) cannot work under the constraints of fear for a long time without suffering the consequences such as illness. Love by its own nature heals. Love is an extremely powerful force and healer. When you love yourself, you heal. When you love other sentient beings, you heal them and yourself. Words spoken with love are healing words. Love does not hold you in a tight grip as fear does. Love, by its own nature, wants to be shared with others. Love looks for unity. Love is Source unifying force. Fear only separates. Fear can be compared to a black hole. It is so dense that whatever falls in it never comes out. There is no sharing, nor unity in fear; it behaves like an infectious disease that contaminates everything it touches and spreads. When Jesus reincarnated, he did it to remind us about the existence of Source love, to steer us toward the energy of love. I will leave you with this reflection.

In love and peace, thank you.

The Crystal Records

Today I have a question for you. Some time ago, I had a vision of a tunnel deep inside a mountain that led to a round space surrounded by four huge, tall, quartz crystals, like towers, I had never seen quartz crystals that big and tall. The space inside the crystals was round and it looked like it was man-made with the purpose of allowing a person to sit inside the circle surrounded by these four crystals. What is its purpose?

You are right in assuming that the space inside the crystals was man-made; it was made in the shape of a circle so that a high priest could sit down and meditate inside this circle. It is a chamber that holds records engraved in the crystals. When the priest sits in the middle of the circle to meditate, everything will start to spin around him and, as a result of the energy field created by the crystals, a door opens that will give him access to the Hall of Records, which is the equivalent of a Source Library of Congress. It is the place where the records of all the lessons experienced by the separate Source sparks are kept.

Now I can see only darkness with pins of light like a night sky full of stars.

Yes, but those pins of light are the actual records. People often say that the records are kept in the Akashic book, but this is not so. That is the human version, one that they can comprehend because it is adjusted to their present reality. You can hardly have a book with paper for all the records that exist if you take into account that yours is not the only dimension or reality. There are many. Those pins of light are the actual records of the events. There are billions, and the difficult part is to find the record you want to check, because you will need permission from your guides and the consent of the souls involved. You cannot use what you see for your own personal gain, only for the good of others. You select a pin of light and then you pull on it until it becomes linear as a horizontal line, and then you just look at it as if it were a video.

So in theory I could go and see the record of who assassinated President Kennedy?

Yes you can, but what good would that do? This person is dead, his family is dead, and the man who killed him is dead. Remember that you can only review the records when you are authorized to do so and for the good of all, not to satisfy your curiosity.

Can you alter the records?

Yes, you can change a record, but that would have an influence on many successive chains of events. It is very complicated to alter records. It can be done because there is no past or future as it is known to you, but all thoughts and actions are linked together like a spider web. If you alter one of the strands, you will alter the configuration of the rest of the strands forming the web. So if you alter the web (the event), it would have repercussions on many levels, and in many other webs.

People have tried to do this?

Oh, yes. Many have tried and are still trying, but only to gain power and control over the future. This is not authorized. To alter the records is not something to be taken lightly. It is not an excuse to shed your responsibilities for the events taking place in your plane.

Let's say that you are polluting the environment at such a fast pace that nothing much will be left for your children or grandchildren to enjoy. You might think that if you went to the corresponding records, you could change the situation and clean the environment. This is not allowed because it would only produce irresponsible beings. Everybody could do what he or she wanted with total disregard for the rest of the beings sharing this experience with him or her. You are responsible for what you create and nothing is going to change that. You would never be allowed to change and manipulate the records this way. All the records are energy and you would have to change the composition and arrangement of those energies to alter the records. In other words, you would have to recreate the event and project the desired image. But if you do not know how to manipulate and change energies, then you would only be creating more records.

I am not too clear on this; can you please explain it again?

The record is created by imprinting energy on what we'll call *a file*. To change that record, you would have to locate it first and then erase what is printed and recreate the event the way you want it to be printed on the file. If you want to change a record without permission, it would be an almost impossible task, with dire consequences.

Remember that this filing system (for that is what the Akashic records are) works very much as your present computer (to put it in terms you can understand). You can create a record, save it, file it, and, once it is filed, you can edit it and file the new version or erase it. The erase command cannot be used with reference to the Akashic records, because you are storing energy and energy is never erased. It can be edited and filed but not erased. To edit, you would take the present energy, reshape it in the form of the sequence of events that you want, and then save it. As I said before, this needs authorization because the editing of records creates a chain reaction in the web-like sequence of interrelated and interdependent events, and it deletes forever the original records of events, but as energy is never erased you will be using the original energy to reshape the events. If you had free access to the Hall of Records, people would change events to suit their own purposes and you would create chaos. Humans are well known for being experts at creating chaos out of order.

Nostradamus was authorized to read the records. He never did it for his own profit. The objective was for him to write a book that would be used to prevent useless grief and sorrow, but most of all the possible destruction of Mother Earth through the use of atomic weapons. His only problem was that, since time is not linear, he pulled records at random and the events he saw were not in sequence, making his interpretation fragmented and misleading.

It is very difficult to locate the records in the sequential way events happen in your dimension. Remember that outside your reality there is no time or space. They are filed at random to protect them from the curiosity of unprepared beings. There are records for all events happening simultaneously in all dimensions and for each individual reality. So you cannot imagine the vastness of it all. When you see a past life, you use these records to see it. But to locate them, you need authorization from your guides. That is why when you saw your past lives, Irene and the rest of your guides were all together in a council to authorize the revision of your records. This is something not be taken lightly. The revision of records can have devastating effects on people who have not reached a certain level of spiritual development (energy vibrating at a higher rate.) There are many people out in your world who say they can assist you with the revision of your records. Do not believe them. You need authorization for this from your council of guides, and authorization is not given lightly. Doctors do it through drugs and/or hypnosis. Hypnosis is like an induced meditation. It suppresses your ego and accesses your soul memory. The soul memory stores all of your personal records. With these methods, you can only access your own personal records, not the Akashic records as a whole.

This is it for right now.

In love and peace, thank you.

Thoughts on Religion

The printed book known as the Bible, and other works, were written by man and are infused with their own egos. Suffice it to say that only man could present God as a man and not as a combination of both male and female. This book contains a lot of wisdom, but man has distorted many of the teachings of Jesus to suit his own interests. The interpretation of these teachings is also done through their egos. The basic concept of any religious teaching is love and compassion for the other beings sharing this experience with you, but, since religion deals with the unknown, man has seen fit to manipulate these teachings to control and instill fear in his fellow man.

The original religious teachings of Jesus have been lost through the many revisions and rewritings of the Bible. Today's teachings are there to suit the spiritual elite and provide them with a powerful tool to control the masses. The concept of a different life after death is totally correct. There is a different life after death and it is totally different from the physical life you are in right now. Life after death is the real life; this physical one is nothing but a teaching class that you have to attend in order to progress in the other life, your total and complete life. This plane is nothing more than a classroom where you can experience the billions of variations that life has. You are here to learn the lessons you set yourself up for (remember this is the objective of your life), and all the other sentient beings here, living and learning their lessons with you, influence each other's beliefs and behavior. Men have learned about fear and how to use it to control. Fear is present in most religions not because it was part of the original teachings but because man put it there so that few could have control over the many.

In many of the stories in the Bible, fear is always present in the image of hell, which is the ultimate price to pay for your wrongdoings. Fear allows a few to have control over millions of their fellow human beings. How can people possibly believe in the power of religions based on discrimination and fear? All religions are the same. Their underlying ideas are good and valid, but the presentation of the teachings has been distorted in order to give its highest members the power to control and manipulate. You do not need to go to a church in order to believe or listen to Source. You are part of Source (as the Bible says that we are made in his image and likeness), and, as part of it, you are Source as well. All of the knowledge, love, and power to transform your world is within you. The power is not outside you.

Prayer is nothing more than a meditation and the chanting of many religions are the equivalent of mantras, but these meditations and mantras are used to separate you from the rest of the beings sharing this lifetime with you. You should be united under one Source, since you are all part of the same Source. Instead, you are led to see yourselves as individual sparks in competition with each other and one spark is better than the other. How wrong!

The concept of reincarnation was suppressed in the Bible during the first council of the Roman Catholic Church, because the men of the time thought that the belief in reincarnation would have made the people unruly and unmanageable. Let me explain to you that reincarnation is not a dispensation from killing and hurting other beings; it is a tremendous responsibility. The knowledge of reincarnation would help people understand that they are responsible for their actions in every single life on this plane. What Jesus said, to treat others as you would like them to treat you, is very true. It is one of the great laws. You could never inflict any pain or sorrow to another human being if you really applied this rule.

If people knew that they could be born as Christians in one life and as Jews in another, as African, Arabs, Chinese, Indian, etc., wouldn't this knowledge change their outlook on life? It would make fighting with each other totally futile. You would only be killing parts of yourself. When you hurt another, you are only hurting yourself. That means being responsible through reincarnation. It is so futile to hate because you would only hate yourself.

When man incarnated in this plane, he soon found that he liked this plane of vivid colors and strong emotions that made everything look so real and vivid—do not forget that this is just a hologram. And he also found that he could play games that gave him power over other beings. He enjoyed this feeling of power that made him feel important, as important as God. Man particularly loves the power to give or take life, and uses this power irresponsibly. To give life is to give opportunity to a spark who is waiting to come to this plane to learn the lessons that it needs to progress in its long journey toward reunification with Source. To take life is inexcusable because it is to take away the opportunity that a spark has to learn its lesson and this will certainly slow its learning process. You have to learn to see yourselves and feel yourselves as a unity where all of you are equal and are only here momentarily to learn your lessons, as if you were going to school to get a degree to make you a better spark. So to waste energy in these squabbles among you is totally unwise. You will just create more lessons for yourselves, making the road toward knowledge much harder and longer.

In peace and love, thank you.

Obstacles and Illness

Negativity is just another manifestation of the same energy. Negativity is not a force in itself, alone and divided from all other forces. Negativity as a manifestation has its own rules. Negative energy, to give it a name that is easily understood, can only manifest according to its nature. These are the laws of physics, but negative things, as they are called in your plane, are not negative. Their nature and their purpose is to force you to take action and learn your lessons, to make you reflect and learn. Remember that this plane is for learning and everything in it is nothing but a lesson. Negative energies are stumbling blocks placed on the road of learning to force you to stop and focus on the block on your path. Whether it is an illness, a setback in your plan, or a sudden loss of comforts and security, these events, when they happen, force you to think, reflect, and go inward into your reserve of spirituality to find out what these experiences mean and what lesson is there to be learned, before you can proceed onward with your life. Until you understand the lessons represented by these blocks, you will not be able to proceed on your path. So reflect when the same events repeat themselves in your life. Look at them objectively from afar and see the lessons in them. Learn them and proceed on the path.

Illnesses are always good teachers. They force us to look at ourselves and to go deeper inside us until we connect with Spirit. They change our usual outlook on life. When you are ill, you often fall prey to despair and it is usually at that moment that you look up to God (in the accepted sense) for answers and explanations. Illness forces us to slow down and examine ourselves and to take time to nurture and heal ourselves. We create our own illnesses not only with our thoughts and deeds in this lifetime, but sometimes we bring them with us from unsolved problems in previous lives. They manifest when our ability to learn stops and our emotions run wild and without control. All the energy created by our wild emotions overloads our circuits and our body collapses, manifesting some illness somewhere. Through illness you learn to appreciate life. You learn to see how fortunate one is when one is healthy and able to enjoy all aspects of life. One learns to pay attention to one's physical body and feel more in tune with it and its needs.

The body is a miraculous machine. It is a universe of its own where millions of actions happen at once to allow you to talk, see, feel, walk, and touch, to be one with your surroundings. When you overload it, it starts showing signs of failure to force you to look at it, to become aware of its presence, and to look at lessons you need to learn before continuing on the path. So give thanks for any illness you have and the lesson that you will be learning from it, because you would never have learned it otherwise. It gives you a chance to learn and to reflect, and you will emerge from it a wiser and more compassionate person.

Nobody goes through illness unchanged and unhurt. The majority of you emerge from it as new beings, full of life and appreciative of your surroundings and with a more acute awareness of Spirit. The minority emerge more bitter and more on the negative end of the spectrum without realizing that their bitter thoughts will only make their health worse and sink them deeper and deeper into despair. People usually turn to their *God* during illnesses that they suffer or someone who is close to them suffers. They pray a lot to their God, asking for solutions to situations that they have created themselves or set themselves up to. They expect God to answer immediately, and when it does not happen they blame God. God has really nothing to do with this. They themselves caused their misery and before the situation clears the need to look at it from a different perspective, without emotions clouding their mind, until they find the jewel in the center, the lesson behind it all. Once the lesson is found and learned, the situation will clear, either by their healing or by their passing on to another plane, because the lesson they came here to learn is completed and there is nothing else for them to do on this plane.

In love and peace, thank you.

Chapter 3

Brief Reminder on How to Manifest

Dalende, people are interested in manifesting, but what they must understand is that they need to stop going back and forth with their thoughts. People need to follow their hearts and concentrate on that instead of going back and forth with their thoughts and intents. They need to establish priorities and follow them until the object of their desire appears in their reality. If they keep shifting your attention, intention, and goals, nothing is going to have the time to materialize.

I have already given all the instructions needed to make things happen in your reality. Use them. Use your visualization skills; feel them as if they were already manifested. Reality, as the book says, is nothing but an illusion. Build your illusion until it becomes your reality. To obtain results, you need to be patient and diligent in your thoughts and feelings. *Do not shift from one set of thoughts to another* because this will erase everything you want to achieve. Keep on the 180-degree path. Go 180 degrees from where you are now, and stay there because everything will start to materialize. This is all for today.

In love and peace, thank you.

What Is Reality?

When your horizon opens and you start to feel and see other dimensions, you lose interest for materialism and this physical plane—sorry, *lose interest* is not the right terminology. You do not lose interest, but your pure physical interest suffers a deep transformation. You start to enjoy life in all its beauty and start to appreciate Mother Earth and all her generosity and beauty. You start to feel more in tune with earth and nature. Physical things tend to fade in the background. Other energies, new to you, start coming into play, and in a way they will expand your views and horizons and make you feel part of the One.

You are part of the One, of all there is. You are all there is. Your reality is composed of many parts; the physical part is not the most important one either. Your dreams, your sensing other energies, the warnings you have received, and the possible future you have seen are your reality. It is a multilayered reality that forms the real you, the true you.

I am so hot.

I know. Your energy level has intensified, but do not worry. It will pass soon.

Your reality is what you think it is and should be. This is a school, and you are here to learn the lessons taught at this school to the best of your abilities.

I have a concept in my mind that I am finding difficult to put into words.

I will help you. Let's try.

I see a tunnel and I am in the center surrounded by scenes from earth. The scenes change according to my thoughts. The important thing is that I am at the center of it. I am the creator of these scenes. I have a feeling of power, of creating what I want to create for my own learning experience and for the benefit of others. It feels like the tunnel of time in the old TV series.

You are correct. There are many tunnels of time, and, as I said before, your reality is different from everybody else's. In a way, your perception of time is different from everybody else's. You are living in your own time at your own pace and learning in your own personal way. There is not one single time applicable to everybody on this plane. There is no such thing. There are many different interpretations of time. The day might be slow for you and fast for another. Time is just a perception to help you live in a sequential way and to give some structure to your physical environment. Indigenous races do not have the concept of linear time you have. Their time is cyclical, governed by the moon and the sun. Is their time longer or shorter than yours? No, the concept and perception of one event are what make the difference.

You are the master of your particular and individual tunnel, so to speak, and you project around you the sum of all your beliefs and fears and, by projecting them, you are in effect experiencing what you have created. It is a hologram, and as it is above so it is below.

You are all sparks of the Creator/Source and, as such, you are able to create the different environments that will allow you to learn your lessons. You all behave as if you had no power to create and as if this power was in somebody else's hand. How wrong. This is not so. Change this perception because it will only destroy you and slow your learning process. You are the center of your universe and you should think and feel as such. There are no limitations but the ones that you impose on yourself.

Enter into your tunnel of reality/life and think. Visualize what you would like to experience as a learning lesson. Let the images spin around you until you get the perfect image, the one that is most adequate to your needs, and focus on it with intent. Do not let it disappear and do not let fear come into play. Nothing is fixed. There are no rules for you to follow. Just follow your heart and what you feel is right. Follow your dreams, because they will come true.

In love and peace, thank you.

The Now and Creation

I was talking with my husband this morning and I told him that the now is everything there is. The past is part of our now (all of our past lifetimes and this) and the future is being built right now. All of a sudden I understood it clearly.

Yes, you are right. Every moment, every instance, counts. It is tremendously important for you to be conscious of every thought and word for they will dictate your experiences in the rest of the nows of your present lifetime. That is all there is in this hologram, the now. It is a moment of consciousness that makes you aware of where you are and what you are experiencing. As I said before, we all live in different realities all the time. What distinguishes one reality from another is your awareness. Right now, you are aware of where you are and what you are doing, and I can assure you that in a short while you will have a different awareness. Focusing is nothing more than being able to keep your awareness alive for a longer period of your so-called time.

Wow. I can feel all this energy going through me. Today it is different. I can feel you on my left side, but I can also feel a different sort of lighter energy all around me. Amazing!

You need some balancing and that is what we are doing. Remember, Dalende, to meditate daily, for that will keep you in balance. It is very easy to be off balance. Meditation is the tool that will keep you connected to your higher self and will allow you to keep your balance.

You cannot teach if you are not centered. A teacher has to keep an open mind and be devoid of judgment and emotions. A teacher is here to help without judging. Always remember it. This is what is wrong with many so-called teachers and churches nowadays. They have strayed from their original mandate. They are all very judgmental and that in itself defeats the purpose of their creation. We are here to share, help, and learn from each other. We are not here to judge one another. Judging is a waste of time and devoid of any purpose. We are all here living the experiences that we have selected for ourselves and this makes judging useless. We are all each other's teachers. Nobody is a better teacher or the only teacher. We all are.

I just had an idea about dimensions. I feel as they are all here and present at this moment.

Every thought and awareness uses different dimensions. The appearance of rigidity and linearity is something typical of this dimension. The majority of sentient beings, here in this plane, do not understand fluidity, so they need to organize everything in order to give an appearance of order to things that do not follow a precise order. Everything is fluid, like waves that flow and superimpose each other; this is how everything is in creation. The beings you call geniuses understand fluidity and use it to create. They are not confined by thoughts of linearity. In the past, their ideas were judged as revolutionary, heretic, and contrary to the established rules, but there was nothing revolutionary or heretic in them. They just followed a fluid pattern of thought, which is much more creative and open than the rigid one that is imposed as a rule. You are open to receive much more information when your ideas and concepts are not linear or rigid, but flow as a fluid would do. Fluidity allows you to go in and out of other dimensions and learn in a much faster way.

I can see patterns of colors and different densities moving in and out as waves and our awareness are nothing more than tapping into a specific wave instead of another. I can see everything moving, flowing in and out with a gentle movement. It is a very subtle matter full of Source. Each particle is Source, and it is full of tiny pinpoints of light and color. Amazing! This is absolutely beautiful. I can see that there are literally billions of different possibilities for life in this environment. Thank you for this vision. I need time to feel it and explore it.

Is there anything else you would like to tell me? There are so many experiences to live out there. I am in awe at the beauty of it all, the simplicity of it all, the magnificence of it all, and the peacefulness of it all. It is a really wondrous creation. Now I know that our heartbeat is nothing more than the heartbeat of creation; it has the same rhythm.

This is why everything is measured as waves. All the energy we generate is measured in waves because it is the fabric of creation.

It is going to take a while for me to come to terms with all this. In my heart, everything seems perfect and simple. Things get complicated only when my physicality comes into play. My brain is trying to make sense of it all, to arrange all of this information in an organized way. My heart just feels it and accepts it all. That is where the connection with Source is, through our hearts, not our brains. Thank you again.

In love and peace, thank you.

Detachment

Today's lesson is on detachment. Remember that this plane is only a hologram and it does not have any real substance. There are only pictures that look real but are of no real substance. Your thoughts give it substance and reality. Reality is not fixed; reality shifts and flows as a wave does.

Sometimes you can be in different realities at the same time. You are in a specific place, surrounded by physical objects, but your thoughts are centered on something away from your present reality and, in effect, you are living for a brief moment that specific reality you were concentrating on. And this happens many times. Nothing is set, static, or predetermined on this plane. Everything is in constant change. Your thoughts and your perceptions change all the time, creating a new and different reality for you to live.

Detachment is necessary if you want to continue on the path of learning. Your ego keeps you attached to this plane; that is its mission. Detachment is a test that all of you need to master on your path to enlightenment. Ego is strong and thrives on emotions. Its energy is kept flowing through emotions. Ego is what keeps you separated from the rest of the (Source) *sparks* and focused on this physical plane. It is only when you recognize the true purpose of ego that you find unity with the rest of the sentient beings sharing this trip with you. It is only by letting go of the hold that ego has on you that you will experience compassion and learn your lessons. Nothing is permanent. Man has been shown this many times.

Many men have lost everything through wars and natural disasters, and life still continues. You will not achieve any spiritual enlightenment or keep your connection to your higher self if you make ego your sole master in this life. You will not achieve anything if you become so attached to your possessions that you become sick at the thought of dying or leaving everything behind.

Why do you think people are always manifesting some illness when they get on in years? Because they are afraid of letting go of their possessions, because they want to hold on to them until the end, and they would like to take everything with them after their death. They are afraid of letting go and of the unknown. This feeling makes them physically ill and the experience of passing on becomes a torment to be feared and endured and not enjoyed as it should be.

You are not what you accumulate and think you own in this life. Those possessions are just the baggage you carry in this life that allows you to travel comfortably from station to station, and nothing more. This baggage does not improve conditions when you reach your final destination. The experiences from the lessons learned are the only baggage you can carry with you, nothing more. Everything that is physical and attached to this plane must stay behind because you are not a physical being. You are light-energy beings and physical items cannot coexist in that context. Everything physical decays with time and renews itself. That is the law of this plane. Everything created here must remain here because it has no life elsewhere. The closer you get to mastering detachment, the quicker you will advance on your path to learning the ultimate lesson. With detachment, there is no ego and no reason to compete, to fight, or to hurt others. There are only compassion and love for everything on this plane.

Learn to detach not only from physical things but also from the physical beings surrounding you, including your family members. Learn to look at them as fellow travelers who have chosen to travel with you during this lifetime and share their experiences with you. You are all each other's teachers. You will meet them again in other lifetimes. Death should be looked upon as the ultimate detachment experience and as a successful graduation into a different experience and nothing to be feared.

In love and peace, thank you.

Coming Earth Changes

Good morning, Knenesset. Anything you would like to tell me? If not, then I would like to expand on my meditations.

So far, I am stuck in the feeling-energy-phase. I can feel my chakras and I would like to learn to direct all the energy toward achieving specific goals. Can I do that?

Yes, you can. Once you are quiet and your mind is as calm as the surface of a lake, so calm as to resemble a mirror, you will be able to focus on the issues that you need help with. Focus on one issue at a time. Reflect its image on the surface of this lake. Ask your guides for help and keep on looking at this lake until you see scenes unfolding in front of you. These scenes will usually contain the answer to the question you asked. If they do not seem to be related to your question, write down what you saw because the meaning will become clear to you with time.

Last night and today I read some awful and disheartening prophecies on events to come, but somehow I am not afraid of what is to come. I just hope to be prepared for the role I am supposed to play in the unfolding of it all. I know that I am supposed to move from here and go west. Why west? I do not know yet, but it will come to me. Where in the west? I do not know either, but it will come as well.

Life, as you know it, will change so much that many people will die of fear—fear of the unknown, fear created by the loss of all their possessions—but this is a lesson long overdue. Man has gone too far in his quest for power. This quest has separated him from his Spirit, his consciousness. He is no longer connected to his higher self, and without this connection he is at the mercy of his emotions and his ego. Ego is not a good counselor. Ego is only the survival tool needed in this plane. Ego was created to ensure the survival of the species; it was not designed to help in the spiritual evolution of man. So this is what is happening right now: ego has taken over and is doing what it knows best, which is the survival of the strongest. It is helping the strongest to survive at the expense of all those other beings and creatures that cannot defend themselves. This is not an ideal state of affairs, as everything is getting out of balance.

The earth and her creatures are out of balance, and this will only create chaos for the rest of the universe, and will have repercussions in many dimensions just as a tsunami has in your world. This is why the moment has come to stop this situation and reverse the flow. Man has to learn the lesson that power is not what really counts on this plane; power means nothing when faced with the forces of nature. What good is it to you to have a bank account with millions of dollars when there is no food to buy, no electricity for your appliances, no running water, no fuel for your vehicles, no insurance to protect your houses, and no insurance to protect your family. It will mean nothing. Millions of dollars will not protect you from what is to come.

This information has come to you to help you prepare for the changes that are coming. Deep down you know that you will be fine. You have been guided until now and we will continue to do so. You already know that you must not settle in the east but need to go west. So you see, your intuition is in tune with our message. The *when and where* will be given to you when the moment is right.

Do not be afraid. You chose to be here at this very significant moment for the beings on this plane. This will be the ultimate lesson in detachment and to teach that you are all one connected in Spirit and with love. You will overcome what is to come. The destruction of all there is on this planet, and possibly beyond it, has to stop. You have not been good caretakers and now you have to pay the price and learn the lesson that comes with the misuse of power.

Power has to be used responsibly, always taking into account the good of all beings present in this plane of consciousness. As you well know, this has not been so. A few people with the only purpose to control others and accumulate wealth in the process have used power selfishly.

The major problem with this behavior is that it interferes with and obstructs the spiritual development of the human race. The major purpose for your presence in this plane is to develop spiritually for the good of all concerned. This is not possible when a few beings control the rest through fear. Living in fear will not allow them to develop spiritually. Since nobody is able to reach this small group of beings because their names, faces, and deeds are not known to the rest, this status quo will never change unless there is a major intervention by the only force on this plane that has more power than all of them: Mother Earth. These people are so drugged with power that they have lost their humanity. They have lost touch with the very essence of their being, and in so doing they have come to regard themselves as gods not accountable to anything or anybody—grave mistake.

All our actions and thoughts are recorded. The energy that we emit through our actions and thoughts is automatically recorded. So you see they are indeed accountable to a higher power for their actions, a player that they never took into account. For all their power and knowledge and playing at being creators, they have forgotten about the real and only Creator of all. Their arrogance has blinded them, and their fate has been sealed. Mother Earth will take over and reestablish the balance before the damage extends beyond this plane.

People have grown to love their power and their possessions so much that nothing but a drastic intervention will change their beliefs and achieve the detachment that is needed. This is their lesson. As I said before, there is a large group of beings whose lesson is detachment. Mother Earth will teach them this lesson in the only way she can, by causing chaos in their worlds and forcing detachment upon them. This will perhaps reunite them with their consciousness and their higher self.

In love and peace, thank you.

Blocks That Prevent Manifestation

Good morning, Knenesset. I know you are around because I can feel you on my left side, so I will go ahead and ask you about manifestation. I know you have given me all the information necessary for manifestation, but I still seem to have some blocks since I am not manifesting what I want. What am I doing wrong?

You have no feelings, no emotions about manifestation. You are too rational. You shift your focus too quickly and don't give any idea time to manifest. You need to center more in looking at what you really want to manifest and then just center on it. Do not be distracted by other thoughts. See yourself as a jogger running on a track toward the finish line. Always keep your pace steady and follow your track and you will reach the finish line. If you don't, and you deviate from the track, you will never make it.

To manifest, you need to follow the same procedure. Keep on your track and run at a steady pace toward the finish line (your goal). Don't let yourself be distracted by the people or ideas surrounding you. You lose energy that way and nothing will manifest. Part of your problem is that you do not know exactly what you want. You keep on jumping from one idea to the next, and in so doing you dissipate the energy needed for creation. We are all here to help you, but you alone can decide what it is you really want to manifest.

Look at manifestation as a new project, a new job. Do not look at the past. Do not think the same way you did in the past because it will only lead you to more of the same. You are traveling on a new road leading in a new direction. Keep an open mind, and you will succeed. Start with a little experiment until you reach your goal. Once you master the technique you will be on your way. You have all the tools. Use them. As I said, look at this as a project you need to complete within a certain time frame. Oh yes, you do need a time frame. If you don't have one, you will lose your focus once again and nothing will come out of it.

Look at this as a lesson in detachment. Once you can manifest what you desire, there is no need for attachment to physical things because they will be there when you need them. There will be no need to keep anything once it has outlived its usefulness. Your life will be uncluttered and simple. Look at it as an energy wave entering your consciousness and leaving again once its usefulness is finished. You receive this energy, transform it into something you want, and then, after using it, you release it again to be used by somebody else. Remember that nothing is permanent, in spite of its physical appearance. It is just energy vibrating at a slower rate. There is nothing to it, Dalende. Do not get bogged down in old thoughts and feelings.

You are still thinking that a person dedicated to spiritual enlightenment should not have the desire for possessions, right? Wrong. You are presently in the physical world, and there is nothing wrong with physical possessions that will help to make your experience here more pleasant. Is Source attached to its creation? No. He enjoys creation in itself and the experiences it provides. Does this enjoyment make Him feel guilty and prevent Him from creating? No. Do you see the similarity?

You are a co-creator, and as such, you should enjoy creating and the experiences it provides. The act of creating is the reason for existence. Look around and what do you see? I see creation, some in line with your vibrational rate and some vibrating at a different rate, but all creation.

Everything present on this plane has been created by a being. The whole purpose of existence is creation and living the experiences it provides. If you do not create, you are not living and you are wasting precious lifetimes. Spirituality is creation and manifestation in this physical plane. Do not deny yourself this experience. Creation and manifestation are part of everything there is. So go ahead and do not feel guilty about it. Always remember that you are a co-creator and create wisely and for the good of all involved.

In love and peace, thank you.

Feelings, Emotions, and Outcomes

Good morning, Knenesset. What are we going to talk about today?

Today we are going to talk about what you were reading this morning. It is not right to say that the universe (all of creation) is made up of tiny granules. These granules are so minuscule that they are almost fluid. It is more correct to say that the universe is fluid, "a thinking and feeling fluid" with the ability to create. In other words, the universe is not static but is live matter. Interesting, right?

The concept that everything has a cause and event and consequence is right. Every event has a cause (prior to the event), and then once the event happens it has a consequence (post-event). So we could say that thoughts or habitual thought patterns lead to specific events and these events will have precise repercussions. I want you to know that nothing is fixed; everything is fluid and moving. The outcomes can be changed, and to do this you only have to change your thoughts and feelings; everything has a probable outcome, not a precise, definite outcome.

You can change the outcome by changing your thought patterns and focusing on your thoughts. Thoughts and feelings are the ingredients of creation. That is what it boils down to. Your thoughts are the blueprints of what you want to create and your feelings are the seed of life—they give life to your thoughts. That is why feelings are so important.

Feelings are not emotions. They should not be confused. Feelings are inborn to everybody who incarnates in this plane. They are part of your genetic code.

Emotions are the result of an imbalance in your feelings and will lead you astray and cause you to be out of focus. Do you understand the difference? Emotions are not feelings. Everybody has inborn feelings. It is natural for all the sentient beings reincarnating on this plane to have feelings. (They are what many people call conscience, master guide, etc.) You all know instinctively when an action you take is right or wrong, but before you can move forward you must consciously choose to acknowledge or ignore the message you feel deep inside of you; it is a matter of free will. You are completely free to do a good deed as you are to do a bad one.

Emotions, on the other hand, are different. Emotions are created by repetitive thought patterns; they are the energy created by a repetitive thought or thoughts focused on only one thing. You focus on one feeling and concentrate on it so much that an emotion is generated and most of the times these emotions run out of control, creating more chaos in your life. Emotions should be avoided at all costs because they will cause you to be out of balance. Feelings keep you in balance.

Everything you are living right now is the direct result of thoughts you had in the past; everything that happens in your life is the direct result of thoughts you had in the past. Do not think of the past as something that has disappeared from your life and has no more direct bearing on your life. That is not so. The past, the present, and the future are all linked and very much alive. All your past thoughts (even yesterday's) are creating your life events of today and tomorrow. If you want to change the events you are experiencing right now, and keep on experiencing repetitively, you have to go into the past and revise your thoughts because they have created what you are experiencing today. Once you come into this realization and see its wisdom, you will understand how everything works; then you will be able to change your present and probable future by going into your past and rewriting the script.

How do you do that? You do it through meditation. Meditation is the golden key to your life. Meditation will give you access to the portal of your lifetimes. Once you are in a meditative state, you can find out what thoughts caused your present experiences and will realize that in order to have a different life (outcome) you must change these thoughts. Be very watchful of your thoughts if you want to create a different future for yourself. Remember to use your thoughts and your feelings wisely.

In love and peace, thank you.

Becoming a Whole Being

Do you remember where you come from?

Yes, I remember the vision I had during a meditation with Irene, but I do not know the name of the place or its location. I know that the place was not on earth.

No, it wasn't. You come from another dimension, more than another planet. You are not from this physical universe. You returned here to help people advance in their quest for spirituality. Maybe we should not call it spirituality but wholeness of being. You are here to show people what a whole being is.

There are many here like you. The problem with this plane is that its beauty, its vividness, and its apparent solidity tends to draw you in, especially if you take into consideration that very few of you remember your origins and past lives when you take on a life here. You came from a dimension that has overcome physical needs and attachment. It is a quiet place where everybody is equal and there are no attachments to material things. Everybody dresses the same, in white, because there is no need to distinguish oneself from the rest since there is no ego present.

Separateness comes from ego. Ego separates to control and create all the little and big dramas present here on this plane. If there were no ego, there would be no dramas to play and no experiences. Everything has a reason. The lesson is to transcend ego and reunite with your whole being. This is what is happening to you. All these energies that you are feeling around you and in you are part of you, and at the same time part of the whole. You are just becoming aware of the *whole of you* and ego is letting you do this because it is learning that it has nothing to fear from your going through this process. Ego is the guardian of this plane. It has to keep sentient beings anchored here and willing to learn all the lessons they came here to learn. If each one of you remembered your previous lives, experiences, lessons, and where you came from originally, none of you would want to remain on this plane. But these lessons are necessary if you want to graduate so ego has to play out its role and keep you here through the attachment you develop for the physical.

Do you know why all those beings that decide to follow their spiritual calling need to be separate from the rest? Because they must work alone if they want to reconnect with their higher self, to become one with their whole being, to feel the energies that make you one with creation, and in so doing become aware of everything that is: to detach from ego and raise their energy levels. You see, energy has its own vibrational level, and it is this vibrational level that will allow you to see and feel things that you normally don't. Everything exists at the same time, right now, at this moment, but you are only aware of a portion of this existence because you are bound by your physical senses. By increasing your energy, you will start realizing the existence of many other dimensions simply because you will become aware of their presence. It is comparable to needing glasses because you see everything out of focus. After you put them on, everything becomes clearer and in focus once again. The same principle applies to energy. On this plane, you are out of focus because your energy vibrates at a low rate. Once you start increasing your rate of vibration through meditation, and the opening of your chakras, you will become aware of a much larger plane of existence. This plane of existence has always been present but out of focus. As your awareness of this new surrounding increases, your focus on this plane (let's say this physical universe) will decrease.

In love and peace, thank you.

Time and Space

Time and space do not exist but on this plane. They are two coordinates used to give dimension and a sense of linearity to this plane. Linearity is needed to locate a period on this plane. In other dimensions, time and space do not exist. Time is totally irrelevant once you are able to observe the overall picture of your lifetimes, and space has no meaning in the realm of multiple dimensions. They are needed in this plane to define your experiences in a particular life because, when you are born, you have no memories of previous lives and experiences. They are used as a reference only.

Dalende, the information you receive has to come from your heart and not your brain. Do not let your ego try to interpret it and make sense of it all, because that will lead to errors and misunderstandings. It has to flow through your heart and your third eye. Your brain does not come into it, as far as interpretation is concerned. Your brain only functions as a keyboard to allow this information to be typed into words. Your brains are not prepared to process information that deals with energy and with multiple dimensions, since you are only using 10 percent of its capacity as it is.

Your education system is exactly what its definition states: a system. It is a system that is focused on using only one side of the brain at a time. This only helps the rigidity of the ideas and views on this plane. Flow is the language of the universe, of creation. Everything pulsates and flows. Everything is alive with energy. If there is no flow then there is no life. The way humans think is wrong. It only stops the flow of energy, the flow of life, which is why everything in your world is dying or sick. Most of you are either sick or dying. You are just reflecting in your bodies what goes on in your thoughts. This plane is made of thoughts and is fed by the energy generated by these thoughts, and, since all your thoughts are generating low energy, this flow eventually stops. This is just a school, and people should view and live their experiences as what they are: lessons to be learned.

In peace and love, thank you.

Linear Thought and Communicating with Your Guides

Part 1 – Linear Thought

Repetitive actions are what make up reality. Reality exists because of your repetitive actions. You play the same actions in this hologram time and time again and that is what gives substance to reality. Day in and day out, you play the same role, perform the same actions, and think the same thoughts. All the energy created by your repetitive actions and thoughts is what makes this hologram real to your consciousness. You follow the same patterns in the physical chores of your days, in and out, as you follow the same patterns of thought. You are so linear that you have invented work to fill your time, work that is also repetitive in its nature. You have created for yourselves a linear hologram where everything follows a linear pattern, and you almost never digress from this norm. The few who have digressed and refused to follow this linear pattern have been the geniuses of all times.

Linear thought is not creative; it will never lead to new discoveries or to new perceptions of life. You are so linear that the major discoveries in medicine and health have all been through luck. Researchers have stumbled on cures for illnesses when they were looking for something completely different. If everybody abandoned linearity as a mode of life and thought, this would be a very different, highly creative plane. Linearity is stable and helps to keep order and control, so it is highly emphasized as a good and wise norm of life. When people behave in a linear fashion, they will never digress from the rules because they firmly believe that by doing so they will create chaos.

The problems of your society right now are caused by the birth of many new souls whose way of thinking does not follow a linear pattern. This creates upheavals and the breaking down of established patterns and rules. Linear patterns are never creative; they provide stability and ensure order and control. Sinuous patterns are creative and lead to the unfolding of new techniques in research and in viewing life. The children born now follow these sinuous patterns. They have a broader perspective of their roles on this plane and how to achieve their goals. Many achieve them even when they have not followed the normal pattern of schooling. Creativity does not need a diploma. There is an immense fountain of knowledge surrounding every being on this plane. It just needs to be tapped and explored, but you will never do it by thinking linearly.

How do you stop thinking linearly? Think of superhighways. Picture the void surrounding your planet as full of superhighways leading into many different directions. You already know that the void is not really void but made up of conscious matter. Everything has consciousness: every atom, every particle. Everything is consciousness, and all its components interact with each other. These *highways*, for lack of a better term, are made up of conglomerates of conscious particles and the way they are linked with each other (the highway) is what you will have to explore to come up with new ideas and solutions. During your meditations, see yourself in space, at a point in space, where many superhighways cross each other. Let yourself be guided and follow the one that catches your attention. See yourself walking on this highway. Look around and observe everything. Observe the matrix of the highway, try to see yourself inside it, and once you are there you will see pictures. Images will come to you. Pay attention to those images, because your answers will be there.

So Dalende, choose your highway and find the answer you have been looking for for a long time. Stop thinking in linear terms. Forget everything you have done so far and concentrate on what you want to do. See yourself standing in the void at the crossroads of all the highways surrounding you and select the one that stands out the most and feels right. Walk on it and feel its matrix. Look at the images and the answer to your questions will be there. Everything is laid out. That is where your probable future already exists. It is only a matter of connecting with it, of feeling it. Right now, you do not feel anything for what you are doing, you are not creating anything, and you are just maintaining the status quo. When you find what you are looking for, everything will change for you and you will create wonderful things. You will then be the master of your own life.

Dependency on work, on people, and on everything that you think is outside you only generates more dependency and your loss of control over the circumstances affecting your life. Only by going within will you connect with your true spirit and regain control of your life. This linear thinking has only served to empower everything external to you and has kept you under control and in ignorance. Your daily struggles create so many dramas that you feel you are barely staying alive. It is like living in a box surrounded by four comfort points—family, work, friends, and money—but it is only a box. Why be satisfied with only a tiny box when you can have the whole universe? There is a whole universe out there for you to explore and lots of building materials for your creations. Reach out and start your life now.

You are not Knenesset, right? Your energy is different. I know that there is somebody else here today with him. Who are you?

I am just another one of your guides.

Thank you for being here with me today.

In love and peace to you both, thank you.

Part 2 – Communicating with Your Guides

Hello, Knenesset.

I always wondered how guides manage to communicate only through energy. We are so accustomed to physical contact that it seems impossible to make contact with another being through their energy field. Amazing! Do you have a physical aspect, or are you just pure, flowing, and vibrating energy?

I do have a sort of physical form. You have seen me.

Yes, you are right, but your form is composed of vibrating energy of a silvery, shining color. How do you communicate with people? How does your energy get transformed into ideas and words?

Dalende, did you forget that everything is energy, that you are energy? Your thoughts and feelings are energy; they are all energy, vibrating at different rates but energy. Energy can merge with other energy. That is how it works.

First, imagine all your body vibrating as energy and feel the energy that you are sending out. The same way you feel my and others' energy, we feel yours. The communication comes because our energies are vibrating at the same frequency, thus making the transmission of thoughts and ideas easy and understandable between us. It is just a flowing and sharing of energies vibrating at the same level. You do not see yourself as energy because you are used to seeing yourself as a physical body. On the other hand, you do not see feelings like love, faith, etc. Many of these feelings are just energy, but you accept them as part of your daily life. It is the same with energy. You have started to accept energy as part of your daily life, so much so, that you are in fact tuning in to me and others with ease. What we are doing is activating certain thoughts and ideas in your mind by using our energies. Remember that nothing is created and that all exists at the same time. We cannot create anything. We just make you aware of its existence. You are doing fine. Communication is coming to you with ease now and it will be even more so.

I wish I could see you.

That is not important right now. The important thing is for you to feel me and for us to communicate with each other.

Knenesset, I know I can feel you, but can you feel me? Let's say I had a problem or needed insight on solving a problem. Can I call on you for your assistance?

Yes, you always can call on me at any time, he said.

How do I do that?

By calling me by my name, I will listen and communicate with you. Call me out loud because my name, as everybody else's, when spoken out loud, has a precise vibrational tone. I will recognize these vibrations immediately and I will recognize them as coming from you because your words will be imprinted with your particular energy. Interesting, ah?

Yes, a whole new world.

No, not new but old. It has always existed and will exist. It is everything that there is, everything that just is.

You are making it easier for us to access your thoughts and communicate with you now. Don't complain about this past year. It was meant to be. You had to follow each one of the steps you did in order to get you where you are now, in order to find the information that would enable you to talk with your guides, and, most important of all, to find two additional guides. We are always with you. Never forget that. Irene was kind enough to serve as the physical link to you. She had to awaken you from your sleep and help you find the path of knowledge you had been looking for for so long.

Try to always keep your energy flowing, your energy field spinning, because this is what allows you to communicate with us and to receive the information we need to send you. This is the reason for meditating twice a day: to keep your chakras vibrating and in working order to receive and send information. Everything is energy and energy travels in many directions. If you stop meditating, your chakras will close down and communication will no longer be possible. Your chakras are like transistors. They enable you to vibrate at certain levels and tune in to the frequencies of each level. So each chakra will open different opportunities of communication because they all vibrate at different rates.

Wow!

In peace and love, thank you for everything.

Lesson from My Mother – Part 1

Good morning, Knenesset. This morning during my meditation, I felt an all-encompassing energy all over my body. I have to say that I have felt it before, but not very often. Actually, I have very seldom felt it as strongly as today.

I can feel this energy on one side of my head. Who is it? You are somebody new, because I have been feeling your energy only since yesterday. Who are you? It feels like there is a whole group of you today. Is this so?

Yes, several of us are here today. We want you to get used to our energies, because we are all going to work with you. We are all members of your family, Knenesset, two others and naturally Irene. You have a lot to learn, but we are all here to help you do it.

You are feeling off center at the moment because your life is going through another upheaval and you are sort of tired of it all, right?

Yes.

It is not an upheaval; it is only another lesson to be learned. That is all. We are all here to learn lessons, remember? Do not get angry, because anger will not help you to solve anything. It will only make things worse and more complicated and you will not learn your lesson. Center yourself by meditating often, as it will help you find the solution you are looking for. We have never abandoned you before and we will not abandon you now. Do not worry; everything will be as it should be.

Do not get bogged down on the same thoughts as you have in the past. They will only create the same feelings of anger and frustration. You know enough now to avoid these emotions, so do not give in to them. Look at them as if they were outside you, from afar. Look at yourself from afar. Analyze yourself with loving eyes as if you were somebody you are interested in. Look at yourself and you will learn your lesson. Look at yourself as a case study. Do not give in to ego ... your ego ... Detach yourself from it.

Your mission is not to go from job to job just to sustain yourself economically. Your mission is to teach; you already know that. We have all told you that. I know you think you are not ready yet, but you are—more than you think. You still have to pass a few stumbling blocks on your path, but you will do so with ease. Give up anger and judgment ... let them go. I know that judgment is difficult to let go because it almost comes naturally to you, since you have an analytical mind, but this is the challenge on your path.

You look at money as the only energy that will be able to support you during this change in your life, but that is not so. This is a way of thinking that is so typical of your plane. Your fear is not letting you think clearly. Give up your fear. Fear only stops the flow of energy. Money is not the only energy that will give you support. The energy that will support you is inside you, not outside. You look at money as being outside you, disconnected from you, and this is not so. You look at the bills that you call money as if they were coming from outside you, and they are not. All the bills coming into your reality are generated by you, either through your work or through your thoughts. They are only an aspect of energy. You have to work with your reality, not your energy. Your energy is fine, but what needs fixing is your reality. You have to expand it.

You have always looked at and felt this money issue as a beggar looks at others for his sustenance. In fact, you have either asked for loans from people or you have been in debt for a great part of your life. Change your reality, Dalende. This is what you must do if you want to change the results. Change your reality and your feelings and the outcome will change. Expand your reality. Look at it as a play and start to play this new game. Everything is a game, a play to be acted, and the situations you live are just lessons to be learned. That is all there is. Do not be fixated on money (the bills) itself. Expand your creativity. Do what you really want to do and all will fall into place.

You still do not know who I am, right?

No.

Think and feel, feel with your heart. What is it telling you?

You are my mother, right? Or should I say the energy that was my mother in her last lifetime?

Yes, that is who I am.

Wow. This is amazing. I thought it was you because of the way you were caressing my face, which is the way you used to do it when you were alive. Thank you for being here and sharing this lesson with me. You have been a good teacher.

Mimmi (my mother's nickname for me), remember that you have to expand your reality. Jobs and loans are not the only sources of income. The energy around you is immense, but your reality is small. You will have to concentrate on expanding it. This is what you have to do if you want to open to other things to come into your life.

In love and peace, thank you.

Lesson from My Mother – Part 2

Good morning, Knenesset. I can feel an energy, but it is not yours. Who is here today?

It is me, Mimmi, said my mother. I am still here.

What happened to Knenesset?

He is here, but he is letting me communicate with you for a while, she said.

So you are still here. How do you feel now?

Great! I feel great and happy. I am very happy to be free of pain at last.

Your death was so sudden that it shocked all of us. It was as if you had voluntarily pulled the plug on your lifeline, and that was it.

In a way, you can say that I did pull the plug out of fear. Fear had dominated my whole life and in the end it had become unbearable and I opted out.

Funny, I always thought that Dad was going to be the one to die first. I never thought that you would be the first one to depart.

I know, but it had to be this way. Your father is the stronger of the two because he is the one with the strongest emotional attachment to this plane. I wasn't too attached. In fact, I had very few attachments, you and your brother and that is it. Even so, I knew that both of you could face my departure without major upheavals in your lives. You have always been strong and independent and away from me for the majority of your life. There was a bond between us, an emotional bond, but even that dissolved itself in the last years of my life. I was your mother, but you were my teacher.

Do you remember that time in Margarita when your father, you, and I sat around the kitchen table to talk about our relationship? That was the day when our emotional bond dissolved and I understood that I was ready to go. You had taught me my last lesson and you had set me free to go. Your brother was always more dependent on my advice than on my emotions. He is more dependent on your father for his emotions. He has always been physically closer to us, but you were closer to me emotionally. As for your father, it was a very difficult lesson to live with him all my life. I chose it as a lesson, but I never completed my assignment. I chose this life to learn about power and freedom, but I departed without completing my assignment, which is why I am still around. I need to finish my learning and the only way to do it is by staying around you so that I can learn from your experiences and your thoughts about our relationship.

You are right to think that our marriage was a karmic one. Indeed it was. It was an awesome lesson that I set myself up for. In the end, fear prevailed. Fear has always been with me, all through this lifetime and others. I was always a very rational being, but the fear I felt was completely irrational. On one side, I inherited your grandmother's fears, and on the other, I added mine to the baggage. I also set myself up for physical limitations, which helped to increase the fear I had of living. Basically, that is what I felt: fear of living on this plane. I did not want to come back, you see, but I had to do it to learn and burn some of my karma. I guess I set myself up for more than I could deal with.

I always admired your strength. You were always strong, even as a little girl. You were not afraid to stand up for what you thought was right. I never could. I know you could never understand why I always took your father's side against you. You have to understand that fear does not help people to think clearly. You do not think with your heart but with your emotions. Your father accepted me with all my limitations and I became dependent on him for my support and protection. I empowered him with my life. The fights came when he felt this power slip away, because you challenged his authority over his family and you challenged his behavior toward me. He saw those two areas as his own domain where a daughter should have no authority. You always challenged his authority and that made him feel frustrated and worthless. I tried a few times to leave him, but I couldn't because I knew that in the end you would find your own way away from me and I would have been left on my own, and I was not ready to live on my own. I did not have the strength to do it. Do you understand now why I did it?

Yes, I do, and I do not blame you really. I do not blame any of you. I also set myself up for the lessons you and Dad taught me and I must say that you were excellent teachers, always unrelenting and very set in teaching me the lessons I had requested. I was just sorry that we did not have time to say good-bye before you departed. It all happened so quickly.

I know, but it was the way that was best for me, she said. I was too afraid and I could not live with fear as my daily companion anymore. I was caught in a loop and I did not know how to break it. The only way I knew was through death. But I am here now. We are talking and I want you to know that I love you very much, and we will see each other again. I will still be around for a while. I am not ready for another lifetime yet. I want to stay here until your father passes on. So do not be surprised if you can still feel my touching your face once in a while. I love you too. Thank you for this lesson.

In peace and love, thank you.

Freedom from Lack

Good morning, Knenesset. I know you are here because I can feel your energy and somebody else's energy as well.

I wish I could finally understand once and for all the concept of wealth. I feel I have been going around the same bush for years and I am still here. What is it going to take to grasp this concept and assimilate it? It should not be too difficult. I know you have tried to help me, but I seem to forget your advice and step right back into the old routine. It is frustrating, but I am stuck.

Dalende, let go. Let go of old beliefs and thoughts and start with a new slate. Can you do that?

I will try.

If you were born today and you had your life in front of you to live as you want, and with the knowledge that you possess now, what would you think? What would be the first thought to come into your mind? Money, it is always around money, and it will always be money if you continue to think the way you have in the past. Why money? What does money represent for you?

Freedom. This is the first word that comes into my mind. Freedom to do the things I really want to do without any constraints.

And what are those things?

I love to travel, meet new people, go to retreats, meditate and share my experiences and help people, and have enough money to spend in my travels without having to calculate prices and how much I have left.

And what is preventing you from doing just that?

The money.

No, it is not the money. It is your will, or your lack of will, which is the real stumbling block in your path to freedom, he said.

Why don't you focus on the problem in a different way? Instead of waiting for the money to come to you to do what you want, why don't you do what you want and see the money come in as a result?

Hold it. I envision myself staying at home, traveling to workshops, sharing with others, traveling for leisure, and my needs taken care of by my husband. How do I go about making this vision a reality for me? Do you see the conflict I have? I see work as the only means of having an income or making money.

When you have a problem, who do you contact first? Your parents, right? Why? Because you trust them and you are certain they will help you. Why can't you trust Source the same way? Source knows it all and can solve it all. Why don't you put your problem, or what you think is the problem in your life, in Source's hands?

Dalende, use your imagination and visualization. Visualize yourself living the life you want and having the freedom you crave. Do not give up on this image. Play it all the time on the screen of your mind. Work out all the details and with time you will see a change starting to take place. You are the maker of your dreams. The life you have had so far was built by your feelings and thoughts. If you want to change it, you will have to start seeing those changes on the screen of your mind and you must feel those changes. It does not matter how long it takes, just keep on doing it. Do not waste so much energy on conflicting thoughts pulling in opposite directions; just focus your thoughts on what you really want, on what is important to you, to your development. Do not give up. Concentrate and focus. Focus on your screen and play your movie. This is the secret.

People who succeed in realizing their dreams have one thing in common: they focus on what they want and do not let themselves be distracted from reaching their ultimate goal. You dissipate too much of your energy in different directions. One day you are going one way and the next you are going in the opposite direction. Stop doing this. Focus on *what you want to see realized* and nothing else. In a way, it is a focused meditation. Leave all distracting thoughts out and just concentrate on your objective and the feelings it creates. Remember that freedom is not dependent on having money, because you can still be a slave with money; you can be a slave to the fear of losing it all. So look again at the concept of freedom that you have, which seems to be dependent on money. Are you seeking the freedom from lack?

Yes.

Ah, but the freedom from lack comes only by freeing yourself from thoughts of lack. The whole of creation is an enormous bank full of creative energy. You only have to tap into Source to be able to create what you want to fulfill your desires.

The only way you are going to change your present situation is through creativity. Be creative, focus on creativity, and believe that you will succeed, and you will. Creative energy has to be felt and nurtured through focusing. Your need to accumulate disappears because you can tap into this energy any time you want and obtain what you need at the moment. This is the real freedom, which is not dependent on a series of events before you can reach it. Freedom is freedom; it means to be free to do as your conscience dictates, for the good of all, without hurting other life forms. If you make your freedom dependent on the possession of money, then it would not be freedom. How much money would you need to reach freedom? How much freedom would you be able to buy? How can you quantify freedom? Freedom either is or is not. There is no middle road. Freedom is a state of mind and not the state of your pocket.

You are the slave of your own thoughts. Nobody is keeping you enslaved but your feelings and thoughts. Change them and everything will change, and that is automatic. Focus on the change, on what you really want, and how you want it in your life. Dare to create what you want and you feel is right according to your conscience. Nobody is placing any limitations on your creativity but yourself. Be creative instead of spending so much time analyzing others, dissipating your excellent energy. Use it to create. Dare to start a new life, to create a new life for yourself, according to your wishes. That is all there is to it. There is no major science involved, no psychology, just your thoughts and feelings. And remember to keep focused always on what you really want.

In love and peace, thank you.

Chapter 4

Energy and Creation – Part 1

Good morning, Knenesset.

Dalende, you are still closed up in your old ideas, aren't you?

Yes. Sometimes I feel like I am running inside a maze, looking for an exit that I cannot find and keep on going round and round searching for it, I said. I know that I need to change my way of thinking, especially my physical way of thinking, but I grew up believing that I was not creative, that I was only an analytical human being, and I have been doing that for a long time now just out of habit. To think creatively is extremely challenging for me. I get frustrated easily and revert almost immediately to my old habits.

All the lessons that you have been patiently giving me make a lot of sense. I know you are telling me the truth, but I still cannot bring myself to be creative, to open up and to trust. It is a battle that I need to fight alone?

Yes, you have been given the tools, but you need to learn to use them and to trust yourself while you are doing it. You are the only one that can change your way of thinking. We cannot do it for you, you know that! Do you remember when I told you that reality is made of repetitive actions? Your reality is made up of your repetitive actions, and if you keep on repeating them, your reality will be the same as it has been up to now. To change reality, you need to input a different type of energy. The same old energy (thoughts) will only produce the same old reality. This is the law.

I feel like I am bumping into the same wall time and time again. What can I do to start developing my creativity? My past couple of lives has not really helped to develop my creativity. Loneliness was my main companion in both of them and the only way to make a breach in this long-standing wall is by the use of pure will.

You need to will yourself out of your present reality. Look at it as an assignment you need to do.

Have you ever given any thought to how you really want your life to be? How do you see yourself living your life at the fullest? Give it some thought. Meditate on it and you will see pictures develop. You should start with only a few ideas, and then in time you will create a great picture full of feeling. And when you begin to live the picture you have diligently created, your reality will change, but remember that if there is no feeling, there is no change. Photocopies have no feelings; originals do. They have the feeling of the person who wrote them. Photocopies are inanimate objects reflecting a reality that has lost its original feeling. When you get into the same routine with no feeling attached to it, you are living in a photocopy of your reality. You need to create an original. Remember this concept because it is important.

Through eons, man has lost his ability to believe that everything that happens in his life is of his own creation. He creates mostly out of fear, but he creates. When you create from fear, you only create hate, division, and power and you help ego to grow out of control. When you create from love, you create union and share the goodness with all your fellow beings, and ego ceases to dominate. Man has become an expert at creating out of fear and has lost his awareness of the other end of the same vibration. He sees it impossible to create using the love energy.

Creation through the love energy has been classified (by all the most widely known and accepted religions) as belonging only to special beings, such as Jesus, Mahatma, and Buddha. These special beings are seen as not belonging to this world and thus not related to us in any way. This is why you have lost your ability to create, because you do not see yourselves as part of these beings, because you have always been taught that they are special, higher in spiritual level than you are, and belonging to a class separate from yours. You have been taught to look up to them, not at them and to recognize yourself in them. You are creators as much as they were. The only difference is they believed in what they were doing. They lived their realities and you don't.

Why is it so difficult for all of you to recognize that you are all creators? You create all the time *out of fear,* but you do create. Once you acknowledge this as a reality, the shift to creating *out of love* should not be too difficult. The main thing to watch out for is your habits. You slip into old habits very easily, since you feel comfortable with them. They have been your companions during all your lifetimes. You know them well.

Look at the new reality you want to build as a construction project. I told you this before: define what elements you want in your picture and just place them there. Nobody can do this for you. Believe in yourself, in your ability to create, build your new reality, and live it. You can always change it if you feel the need for it.

Remember the only rule (since you will be using the love vibration) is to do it without harming others. Always let love and compassion dictate your actions and leave your ego aside. Talk to your ego and make it understand that it can leave you alone, that you will be fine without its guidance for a while. Tell your ego that it can trust you, that you are not going to do anything that will harm your being. Tell it that it can relax its guard for a while. Use the following affirmation to talk to your ego.

Say, "Ego, I love you and thank you for all the years of loving vigilance and care. I release you right now of your duty in love and peace. Do not worry about me because I will be fine. Nothing bad will happen to me while you take a well-deserved rest. Do not worry about me because nothing is threatening me right now. Be assured that I will call upon you as soon as the need arises. Thank you."

I now release all my fears of lack in a bubble of pink (for love) and violet (for transformation) light. These fears are floating away from me as I speak, never to return. I replace them with feelings of joy and trust in the abundance that is already in my life. I am a creative being, part of the whole creation, and as such empowered to create everything I need for my highest good. Thank you, guides and guardian angel, in love and peace.

Dalende, do you remember that room at Disneyland where you were surrounded by huge screens all showing the same picture (panoramic screens)? That is what this dimension is that room is very similar to how this earth hologram works. You are surrounded by the images of your life. Your thoughts make up the pictures, your reality. If you want the scenes to change, you have to think and feel differently. It is as easy as that. Your thoughts will change the scenes. Picture the new scenes the way you intend them to be. Do it time and time again until this repetitiveness creates your new reality. This is not too difficult, is it? You only need *will*. Remember you have to will it for it to become your reality. Will is what keeps us in the now, and the now is where we build our reality.

In love and peace, thank you.

Energy and Creation – Part 2

Hello, Knenesset. Is there anything else you would like to tell me now?

Yes. You have to do this exercise. Go to your panoramic room, the one surrounded by all the screens, and start imagining how you would like to live your life. Once you start, the rest will come to you easily. Build on your initial image and you will see how your creativity will start flowing.

I can see everything spinning around me. The images are going by very fast.

That is the energy of creation; everything spins at fast speeds because energy cannot stay still. Energy vibrates all the time and there is no stillness in creation. Stillness is an illusion of the physical being. You would not be able to function on this plane without the concept of stillness. But there is no stillness as such in creation. Once you start to have thoughts on what you want, your reality will start to create images and the spinning will slow down and then stop. Then the appearance of stillness will be in place. By spinning, sparks are thrown out from Source and once they complete their rotation, they return to Source. So all of creation emanates from Source, and it will come back to It once the cycle is complete. So are all beings through their reincarnations. When, through all your incarnations, you learn your lessons, your energy will vibrate at different rates in each incarnation. When you are ready to return to Source, your vibration will be much higher than when you started on this journey. Source is everywhere because its sparks are everywhere in creation.

You have read about the Merkaba. Well, the Merkaba spins, right? It is through this spinning that the Merkaba travels to other dimensions and times. Spinning is a major concept in creation. The energy of the chakras spins, so you see the spinning concept is everywhere because energy is everywhere and energy vibrates and spins. Stillness does not exist. When your reality stays still, you feel trapped and frustrated because nothing is moving on. Stillness is not good for beings here on this plane. Stillness kills creation, and you create with your thoughts and feelings. So spin those thoughts and feelings and you will create wonderful things.

In love and peace, thank you.

How Your Thoughts Shape Your Life

Good morning, Knenesset. How are thoughts converted to the reality we live? For example, right now I am communicating with you through my thoughts. I am not speaking. How am I receiving your information?

You are receiving it through the transfer of energy. Remember once again that everything is energy; keep this in mind. Absolutely everything is energy, which has its own frequency and vibration, and these determine the difference between thoughts. Everything manifested on this plane has been in thought form before manifesting. Everything manifested represents somebody's thoughts. Everything you have manifested so far in your life was in thought form at some time. Let's take the example of your work. You already knew when you started working that the company you were working for would not last more than a year. You affirmed it so many times, remember? Well, it has manifested. The demise of this company is nothing more than the manifestation of the thoughts of all the people working for this organization.

You wanted to come to this city, because you liked it more than any other. You affirmed it time and time again, and here you are! You determine through your thoughts what your future (that in reality is not the future) will be for you. You build your road (the future) with your own thoughts, which are the building blocks and the future is nothing more than the manifestation of your thoughts.

So let's go back for a moment to a subject that is very important for most beings: money. Examine all the thoughts you have had on the matter. You always thought that you needed to work, and you have. You always looked at your jobs as the only means that money could come to you, and they have been. You never thought of doing something different from having a job. You never saw yourself as deserving of receiving money, or anything else for that matter, and you haven't. Your thoughts of lack have been the cause of the debt you had in the past, because you never saw yourself as deserving lots of money. You always thought that somebody on the spiritual path was not entitled to enjoy the comforts that money can provide. Can you see the pattern?

Do you understand what I am trying to say? You, and only you, through your thoughts, have caused all the lessons that have manifested in your life. In doing so, you have fallen into a vicious circle on the money issue. You have been thinking along the same pattern for so long that you cannot contemplate a different way of thinking. Making things happen, it is as easy as changing your thoughts.

There are no special formulas, and beware of those who tell you otherwise. These beings are so creative that they are making their fortunes by selling you their ideas of how the system has worked for them. Remember that this does not mean that it will work for you. Different thoughts create different realities. So the ball is back in your court. Do you want to see changes? Then you must make them happen.

Luck per se does not exist. People who are seen as lucky make themselves be lucky; they believe in luck. If you don't believe in luck, really feel lucky, nothing will happen. What do you want? What is it that deep down you feel comfortable with? Think about this for a moment. You really like staying at home, you like meditating, you have been writing your lessons, you enjoy cooking, you enjoy traveling, you would enjoy having a house surrounded by mountains, and, most of all, you enjoy doing all this in a leisurely way.

Remember that year when you stayed home from work? It was the year you enjoyed the most. It was a great year for you. You did what you enjoyed doing: being you. Now you have to plan your life the way you intend to live it and use your thoughts as the building blocks for its realization. This might take some time because old habits die hard, and ego is always present to tempt you to follow the old familiar ways. But I will say it again: nothing is going to change unless you will it to change. You are not a competitive person. You do not enjoy working in an office environment; you only enjoy the social side of it. Why go to all the trouble of finding another job that will only impose demands on you if you do not want to live your life this way? It does not make any sense. You have been given the tools to change your life, but the changing is up to you.

Dalende, there are no preset patterns to somebody's life. You come here with certain lessons to learn, but the way you set the stage up to learn them is totally up to you. Most people get so involved with setting up their stage that they miss the purpose for the setting of the stage and get lost in the details. You are a creator, and as such you always create, sometimes out of fear, sometimes out of love, but you are always creating. Start writing down all your thoughts on how you want to set up your stage; keep on thinking about this new stage and you will see how your present stage will change. Do not think about anything else; do not pay attention to anything else. This is your life, your stage, and at this point you should know how you want to live it. Do not give in to other people's thoughts or ways.

Convention and conformism do not exist but on this plane. They were invented by those unable to create. There would be no need for rules if all beings lived connected to Source. There was a great truth in what Jesus said: treat others as you would like them to treat you. I would add this:

love others as you would like them to love you. Beings on the spiritual path cannot stray from living by this rule; it comes with the territory. So go beyond the rules, forget about them, because you will not break them anyway. You cannot break them, for the path you are on will not allow you to do that. Create what you really want; all the rest is just an illusion.

In love and peace, thank you.

Do Not Let Fear Enter Your Thoughts and Feelings

Good morning, Knenesset.

I have noticed that even when I ask you the same questions over and over again you never get upset and always have an answer. Amazing!

Emotions belong only to humans. No other race anywhere else in creation has so many emotions as you do. Emotions reflect the beauty of your surroundings. Everything on this plane is so intensely physical that it had to have its correspondent in the intangible. That is how emotions came to be. The downside is that emotions do not allow you to think clearly. They make you react violently and lose your objectivity. In order to make the right decision, you should look at a situation without any emotions, as if you were looking down at a movie from above, where you are not a participating actor but an observer. This is the only way you will observe all the dramas and lessons playing in the scene that you are looking at. Once you get involved, you lose your objectivity because your participation will force you to play a role and take sides.

You are here to learn, but learning in the best possible way, not learning by suffering and making your lives miserable. This is the wrong way of learning. When you learn out of fear and hate, the lessons tend to repeat themselves because of the violence of the emotions involved. The energy of these emotions hangs around you like a fog, involving you in its mist and blinding you. When you are in this dense fog, you cannot see beyond it and the fog will never dissipate. When you learn out of love and compassion, there is no fog and the path in front of you is clear for you to see and follow. That is why it is so important to love and share this love with all other beings. Love generates more love and erases hate and fear. Fear should be erased from your thoughts and feelings. Fear is the most damaging of emotions, because it blocks the flow of energy. When you operate out of fear, your energy flow stops and creativity is destroyed. It is destroyed in the sense of having the ability to create positive and loving images. Creativity continues in the form of having the ability to create images based on fear that will only increase your fear and block even more your energy flow.

The blocking of your energy flow generates all sorts of problems, both physical and spiritual. Physical energy blocks lead to illness, and spiritual energy blocks lead to desperation and frustration. The one thing that you must remember from this lesson is this: *do not let fear enter your thoughts and feelings.*

Always try to think of love and compassion and the problems in your life will disappear. It is as easy as that. Remember that fear blocks energy, and, since everything is energy, you are actually blocking absolutely everything from entering your sphere of energy and manifesting. There is nothing to be afraid of. You are always supported in loving care. Remember that Source creates out of love; Source vibrates at such a high rate of energy that it is beyond light. At such a high rate of vibration, negative emotions cannot exist as they vibrate at a much lower level, thus creation can only be positive and out of love. Remember that at this vibrational level the positive contains all negative. The negative is absorbed back into Source without touching it because its vibration, by its very nature, is lower than Source's, but it is contained within Source. So whatever you do, never be afraid.

Fear is a damaging emotion and of no use to your progress. Never think, feel, or act out of fear. It will only create more fear. It will only reproduce itself, and the fog will intensify around you until you will be unable to follow your path. What is there to be afraid of when you are surrounded by so much love? But love cannot be felt if you block its energy with fear. All children when they are young trust their parents implicitly. They never question their actions and they love their parents even though some are mistreated very badly by them. This is the love that is in them, the love that comes from Source that has not yet been touched and contaminated by fear and hate. Later, when all the children undergo the external conditioning that is so familiar on this plane, they lose the spontaneous and natural love they brought with them at birth and the cycle starts all over again. They lose their connection to Source. This is what the Christian ceremony of baptism is: the symbolic reconnection to Source-Spirit that we lose after birth. Actually, we do not lose the connection with Source-Spirit at birth but a few years later when the conditioning from the grownups sets in. The child's innocence is nothing but pure love and it should be respected and nurtured, not changed and chained. The problems of humanity all start with the education of their children. But this will be the theme for another lesson.

In love and peace, thank you.

Feelings and Emotions

Dalende, I just want you to know that I am always with you. Even when you do not feel me, I am here with you. This is one of the most intense, vivid planes to reincarnate because feelings here are so strong, and the emotions they create are very powerful and long lasting, but it is a necessary step in the learning process on how to develop your whole being. Once you manage to graduate from feeling these feelings and strong emotions, you will be on your way out of this particular plane. You will graduate to a higher class.

When you feed off emotions, the lessons become complicated and you create a lot of turmoil for yourself. Learning how to deal with emotions should be the first lesson to be learned by all the beings here. This is the plane where fear is predominant, where most emotions are generated by fear, but I have already told you that. Things would improve dramatically if everybody forgot about fear and worked out of love. Fear is generated by your desire for security. You all want security so badly that you try to predict all the future possibilities to prevent events that would cause you pain and sorrow. You do not look at these events as lessons but as tragedies, but in every tragedy there is a lesson to be learned.

Imagine yourself as an actor playing a role. All your emotions are concentrated in playing this role to the best of your abilities, so much so that actors find it difficult coping with their own personal lives once they finish playing their roles in a play. There are actors who take drugs, drink, and behave abominably, because some of the emotions they act out and feel, while playing their roles, remain with them and become part of them, and they feel the need to heighten or dull their feelings. The best course of action is for you to play your role, keeping your emotions under control and looking at yourself from a distance. See yourself through a camera lens while you are playing this particular role. Always remember that when you feel strong emotions, you radiate lots of energy, usually strong negative energy. This energy only creates more problems for you, since all the thoughts you create, when under this condition, will be overcharged and will only create more strong emotions until you will be caught in them as in a spider's web, and everything will look blacker than it actually is. When you find yourself in a situation where you are in the middle of this vortex of energy, give yourself the gift of a short meditation to restore your balance. Cut all your ties with these emotions and you will see how everything calms down and changes. If you keep on feeling these negative energies and use them to create your thoughts, you will only create a lot of problems for yourself, and you will gain nothing but frustration and sorrow. You must change your perception of the events in your life. This is what makes all the difference. Your perception is what makes the difference in the way you live your particular reality.

You already know that reality is different for everybody since you all have different perceptions of the same event. Your life is only your perception of it. Nothing will change until you change the way you perceive your reality. This is all there is. This past year has been excellent for you. You have come a long way. You were given the time and resources to find important and useful information. You have connected with two of your guides and you have started to write about these connections. This should show you that everything happens as it should, and for your highest good. You could not have achieved everything you have so far if you had a more demanding job. Your stress levels would have increased and that would have been detrimental to your health.

You will be guided once again toward the right path. Do not worry. Everything will fall into place at the right time. Your only responsibility will be to exercise your free will to recognize what that place is. Both your intuition and connection to your higher self are excellent, so you should not have any problems. Let yourself be guided by them. Always listen to them.

In love and peace, thank you.

Creating What You Desire

The hang-up that a great majority of beings seem to share on this plane relates to the creation of money.

Money is not what will make a person happy. Money on its own does not have any particular meaning. It is neutral. Money takes on the meaning that people are willing to give it.

There is a lot of truth in the saying "do what you want and the money will follow." People need to focus on what is that they *really* want to do. The must have this idea very clear in their mind. As I told you many times before, if people keep on being undecided on what they want to do, then they will create and destroy all the time, so they will always remain in the same spot, not moving forward or backward. You all have a very powerful mind, but you have to learn to use it in a positive way. Start by working on the following:

1. writing down what it is you want to do;
2. how you see yourself achieving this; and
3. opening up to the creative energy around you so that creation can take place.

This sounds good, but I do not understand how I am supposed to open up to the creative energy around me. How do I do that? What exactly is this creative energy?

Creative energy is just energy, like the energy you feel when I am communicating with you. The only difference is that creative energy vibrates at a different frequency.

- ❖ First, you have to see yourself and picture yourself as the Creator.
- ❖ Imagine that you have all the power and tools you need to create.
- ❖ Feel free to think about all the things that give you happiness and pleasure.
- ❖ Let your imagination fly without any inhibitions and limitations.
- ❖ Forget for a moment all the inhibitions that were planted in your mind by your parents, education system, TV, magazines, books, etc. because they are restrictions created by man to control man. (If man was allowed to create what he wants and feels is his birthright, there would be no need to work, to purchase, to accumulate. The actual economic and religious systems would automatically collapse, because there would be no need for them.)
- ❖ You are *all* there is.
- ❖ When you create your pictures, feel them deep inside. Feel the emotions that they produce. Feel these emotions deep in your heart and solar plexus chakra.
- ❖ Keep doing this, adjusting your images, as you work with them, for as long as needed for creation to take place.
- ❖ Remember that images are like clay; you can mold them and remold them as you wish. They are not the ultimate product. You need to work with them and refine them until you get the product that you really desire deep in your heart.
- ❖ Do not give up on this. If you want to create, you need to stay focused. Do not get distracted by other things. Keep working on your blueprint and you will succeed. This is all there is to it. No matter how many books have been written on this subject, these are the steps needed to create.

Creation and manifestation only depend on the amount of creative energy and emotions that you are willing to put into them. If you are not willing to invest time, effort, and feelings, nothing will happen. Remember the Bible states that creation took six days. There is some truth in that. Creation on this plane is not instantaneous. It takes time, or what appears to you to be time. Remember that the concept of time does not exist anywhere else but here. Time is only used to designate an action that is defined by having a beginning and an end. If it did not have a beginning and an end, it would not be an action and it would not stand out on its own. It would be part of chaos.

In love and peace, thank you.

Thoughts on the Principles for Creating and Manifesting Your Desires

At this moment, you are all living the experiment you have created for yourselves. Emotions create. You use emotions and thoughts to create. They are alive with energy, thus they can create. You are an experiment in process. Having been generated as sparks by Source, and having become physical (thus forgetting your origin), the experiment is simply to observe, if you can, from this physical plane and, while oblivious of your origin, return to Source.

You came here to heal your relationships from the past (i.e., your father), to teach strength to your mother, and to live your life with Tony, as planned. You have been a teacher to your children. You have been a source of strength to all those around you. Do you know what your highest purpose is now? It is to love all of creation with no reservations, to feel compassion and not pity. You still need to put a few things in order. You are on the brink of discovering your true self. This is your major lesson in this particular life. Your true self is the result of all the lessons learned through your many reincarnations and you must recognize that you are also a spark from Source, and as such you are one with the rest of creation. You are just beginning to recognize and feel this.

I am going to give you an example. Let's say you have lived a great part of your life struggling financially, which means you have been struggling with the concept of lack for many years and you want to stop this continuous struggle and obtain abundance. First of all, we must define what *abundance* means for you; you must define this concept clearly first, because abundance refers to many things like money, health, love, and work. For this example, let's assume abundance refers to money. Does it mean receiving a certain amount of money in one lump sum? Is it receiving monthly payments (for a job)? Is it receiving an unexpected income? Is it being able to create what you want when the need arises?

For me, abundance is being able to create what you want when you need it without obstructing someone else's free will. Nothing else is needed when you reach this point.

Now that you have defined what you really want, he said, let's continue with this example. The result you want to achieve (creating what you want when you want) is the mass. The fact that you are struggling financially is the velocity. A change in momentum must occur if you want to manifest abundance. If your purpose is to end your financial struggles, but if you keep on thinking, feeling, and willing for the situation to end, allow me to say that it will not end! Why? Because your complete focus will be on your financial struggles, and if you continue to focus on these they may even get worse! To ensure a successful outcome, you must immediately shift your focus to abundance! When you think and feel abundance, you are creating a shift of 180 degrees from your belief in lack and now your focus has nothing to do with lack. You are focusing on the opposite of lack. Lack would cease by destructive interference. In other words, it would cancel out, and with more time of applied force (focus) it would become abundance by constructive interference.

Your intent is your force. How long you are able to sustain your intent is your time. If you are poor, do not focus on being poor but focus on being wealthy. If you are you sick, focus on health. If you are you angry, focus on peace. If you are you afraid, focus on love.

Do not keep shifting from one state of lack to a state of abundance, from a state of sickness to a state of health, from a state of anger to a state of peace, and from a state of fear to a state of love, because you will achieve nothing this way, and you will only waste your precious energy. If you really want to change the situation, remember that you need to focus your attention 180 degrees in the opposite direction of what you are experiencing right now, and sustain your focus until it manifests. If you keep shifting your attention from one state to the other, you will only create a whirlpool of energy and nothing will manifest because there would be no force and no focus. The universe and its energy are part of you. You are part of creation and the Creator, and as its spark you can create whatever you will.

Whatever you believe in, whether out of love or fear, that is what you will experience in your life. You are always drawing the blueprint of your life, of your experiences. Fear is as strong an emotion as love. If you believe in fear and create out of fear, you will get what you believe in because Source can only give to itself what he is asking for (you are part of Source and as such are Source). Your free will determines what experiences you will live.

Money in itself is nothing more than an object as a car, a house, a boat, etc. Money does not have a feeling of its own. Whatever feeling you associate with it, this will be the feeling it will have for you. Most of you have attributed to money a feeling of power that it does not have. You are the one holding the feeling of power; it is your own perception. Money is an object, a hologram that does not have any feeling of its own. Your perception of it is what makes all the difference. Thoughts of lack will only increase its manifestation in your life, but if you shift these to thoughts of abundance for an extended period of time, until you truly believe in abundance, this new belief will destroy the present unwanted situation. In other words, it is the healing energy.

So many ideas and concepts are put out into this reality at every moment that it is almost a miracle for anything to survive such an assault. Love is so powerful that the energy of the very few sparks of pure love that came to this plane thousands of years ago are still alive today (Jesus, etc.)

In love and peace, thank you.

Energy, Fear, and Love

Good morning, Knenesset. Today I am happy. I do not know why, but it is a wonderful feeling. The day is gorgeous and I am happy to be alive, or should I say to be conscious of living in this hologram.

Last night while I was meditating, I felt so much energy that suddenly I felt as if I was this energy and my body were just one shape with no life of its own. It was really strange. I think that we have it all wrong. The real us is not this body we carry around on this plane but the energy that we feel and are. The body is just a mold where all the energies we feel through our emotions and thoughts are imprinted.

Thoughts and emotions are energy and as such they have a life of their own. When we die, we will be judged not by our actions but by the thoughts and feelings we had at the moment of our actions. Everything we have thought and felt in our lives will be presented to us and we will be the judges of everything we have felt and thought. We will feel again the impact that those thoughts and feelings had on us and other people. This is the real judgment. Nobody is going to sit in judgment of us but us. This is why you should always be careful and vigilant of your thoughts, because they will come back to you after death.

Everything we think and feel is reflected in our bodies and environment. We mold our bodies and our environment with our thoughts. This is why there are millions of realities being lived at the same time on this plane. Every one of us has a different and personal perception of reality. As soon as we are born, our parents start telling us how much we resemble one of them, and when we grow up we reflect it. We all look a bit like our fathers or mothers, but we do not have to. We are ourselves, our own individual energies, not bound by thoughts and feelings. Our parents were just the vehicle that allowed us to access this plane. The only access to this hologram is through the people already in the hologram. Nobody can access this hologram directly, because a preset condition for being here is to forget everything about our past experiences and lives. There would be no point in participating in a game where the outcome is known from the start.

We are not bodies but energies molded in a body. We need to have a body in order to be in this dense, physical plane. If we kept our original nature of energy, nobody would be able to see us. We would be here, but we would have no way to communicate or experience anything. Where does the fear that is present in this plane come from? Why do most people operate exclusively from fear?

It is all part of the experience game, Dalende. In order to ascend, you have to be exposed to fear as well as love. If all your experiences were based totally on love, the range of experiences for Source would have been much more limited. Love allows for a faster ascension. However, by widening the range of experiences to include fear, the road to ascension will be longer because it allows for many more experiences to happen so Source can have a vaster array of experiences for a longer period. The road to ascension will be slower, because you have to consciously realize that you have to overcome and transform fear first. Some beings realized early on that by using fear they could manipulate people and gain control and power, and power is a very strong emotion. This is why so many beings are still stuck in this emotion. It makes them feel close to God, because they think of God as a manipulator who exercises power over them. Wrong, totally wrong. Also, do not forget that these beings were placed here with just that purpose: to instill fear in other beings, to see what experiences this generated, and to see if the beings playing in this drama would be able to transcend and transform their fears into love and start their ascension back to Source. The problem is that you all have been caught up in this game and the emotions and thoughts involved in it are so powerful that they are difficult to overcome.

This plane was created to be very intense, in colors and emotions, with the sole purpose of creating attachment. On the road to ascension, one of the main lessons you must learn and master is how to overcome attachments. Free will has to be exercised to overcome these attachments. Many beings are like fish caught in a net. They are caught in the net of fear and attachment and cannot find a way to escape these feelings. Don't forget that the net is only an illusion. Once you understand that all there is on this plane is just an illusion generated by your collective thoughts and emotions, you will start to walk on the path to ascension. Remember that this is just an illusion and you can change its parameters any time you want. You are the creator of your own experiences. Nobody and nothing is forcing you to live a life you no longer desire. This has to be very clear. You are the creator of your life, of every experience, illness, joy, sorrow, etc. You set yourself up for everything you experience with your thoughts and emotions.

In love and peace, thank you.

Generating Energy to Meet Your Financial Needs and Learning to Receive

Dalende, first of all, you must understand that money is an energy that is not separate from you but it is an energy that is part of you, as everything else is. Money is an energy that is as part of you, as is love, hate, compassion, pity, etc. You have grown accustomed to seeing money as a separate force that has power over your life, over the way you live your life. You have empowered this idea with so much fear and negativity that nothing good comes when you think about it. Money = Fear. You have lived your whole life by applying this equation. It has not worked out, and it never will. Since you have associated money with fear, you will always handle all the situations involving money with fear. The two have become so attached to each other in your thoughts that you will need to retrain yourself consciously, otherwise you will continue to go around in an endless circle.

How can I overcome this and change the programming in my mind?

You can change it by applying will. You have to will yourself out of this never-ending circle, he said.

I know. I am quite clear on that, but where do I start?

You must start with your feelings. Every time you think about money or handle money, you must switch your feelings from fear to love and joy. Think about all the joy this wonderful energy is giving you every time you buy or pay for something, every time you exchange it for something you want. It is always there for you. If you analyze this, money has always been there for you, either to pay for things you needed and wanted or for you to receive. The only problem is that it has been there for you in the form you have always thought about and asked for, with fear and in debt form. Now that you have come into the realization of why this was happening, you are consciously ready to change and ask for what you think you now deserve. Do you really believe you deserve to receive money with joy and love so that you can have the life you want to live? If the answer is yes, then nothing can prevent you from reaching your goal. You set your goal, and you must also set your thoughts and emotions to match your goal.

Dalende, you have to do this consciously in order to change the outcome. Your fear in dealing with money is so engrained in you that you automatically think, feel, and work out of fear. In order to change this, you have to make a conscious effort to change. You have to live in the now. Be conscious now of your feelings about this energy. Do not let one bill, one coin pass, through your hands without thanking it and feeling love and joy for its energy and the energy it allows to enter your life. This needs to be done all the time if you want to change your feelings.

Actually, the freedom you associate with having plenty of money does not come from the money itself; it comes from deep inside you. It comes from your ability to tune into this energy when you need it. This is the ultimate freedom. In order to achieve this, you have to work out of love, trust, and faith. Never give in to fear, never work out of fear. This will only create problems and more lack. The feeling you need to generate is equivalent to the feeling you have regarding finding a job. You said that you have always been able to find a job when you needed, and it has always been so. The same principle applies to money. Money is energy and unless you believe that money will always be there for you when you need it, debt and fear will always be with you. You have no doubts about finding a job when you need it, then why do you have all these doubts regarding manifesting money? It is only energy. Once you get rid of all your doubts and fears, things will change. You will start manifesting what you feel you want and are ready to receive. This is another important aspect of dealing with money energy.

For some people, it is easy to give but difficult to receive (including you). This prevents the smooth flow of energy. You should be able to feel joy in receiving, not just in giving. Giving is great, but receiving is its complement. Giving and receiving together form the circle of flow. There is nothing bad in receiving or in giving. In many of your past lives you were used to giving. You enjoyed giving and this was a great lesson for you, but in this one your lesson is to learn to receive with joy and love, not with shame and fear. There is nothing shameful in receiving. I wonder where you got that idea from. Receiving does not automatically mean that you are lacking something. Receiving is only the exchange of energy with a person who cares for you and gives out of his or her love and affection for you. It is a loving exchange of energy.

Break the boundaries of the prison you have set up for yourself. It is time for you to be free, to enjoy the freedom that you picture on the horizon. This freedom has to come from within you. Nobody can set you free but yourself. So start working and stop wasting precious time. You have all the tools you need. Use them, but I cannot force you to use them. It is your free will.

In love and peace, thank you.

Energy, Its Frequency: Meditation

Good morning, Knenesset. How do you communicate with me? I know we are all energy, but how does energy transform into thoughts?

Dalende, how do you think? I think mostly in images and sometimes in words.

Feeling is what makes thoughts real to you. You can think all day and night, but if you do not feel (from your gut), your thoughts are like words written in white on a white sheet of paper: nothing will come out of them. I communicate with you through images you understand and sometimes through words. The secret lies in the frequency of the energy. Imagine a huge library where all the information is energy that is stored by its frequency. Everything is energy, but what differentiates energy is the frequency. Everything, absolutely everything, has its own specific frequency. The frequency is what determines the type of thoughts (images) you receive and generate. Love has a different vibrational frequency than fear.

It is a very complex subject. Beings are always thinking and generating thoughts and all these thoughts have their own frequency, and thoughts of the same frequency are attracted to each other. This is why miracles happen. When a group of sentient beings is on the same frequency, it can change the now, and the apparent reality. This works for what you call good or bad. Remember that there is no good or bad. These are only two extremes of the same energy, and this energy could not be aware of its existence without its two extremes. What defines the existence of energy are the extremes that are contained in it.

Energy just is. It is everywhere and contained in everything. It is an emission of Source. How would you realize the existence of this energy if you could not differentiate it? If it was not differentiated, you would not be aware of its presence. By differentiating it, with the existence of good and bad, right and wrong, love and fear, etc., you are giving it dimension. You are making it a participant in your world of reality. You become conscious of its presence.

At your stage of development, you do not see energy as such. You can only feel it. The time will come when you will be able to see the energy around you and see its vibration and color and be able to determine its frequency. At this point, you can feel the frequency when somebody resonates with you or not, but you cannot go beyond this feeling yet. There is so much for you to learn and see. As you know, nothing is separate. We are all one, because we are all part of the emission of Source and we are part of the energy of Source. We all have the same characteristics and are made of the same basic material. Our individuality is in our awareness of it. You can be aware of it or not. You are all living in this reality, but with different degrees of awareness.

Meditation

I have a question for you on meditation. When I meditate, I can feel all these energies, but I do not go beyond this feeling stage. I do not think that feeling energy is the sole purpose of meditation.

No, it is not. Energy is the first step on the meditation path. By feeling the energy, you become aware of your oneness with all there is. You lose the feeling of separation. Once you lose that feeling of separation, you are ready to go beyond and seek the truth. Do not work alone. Always ask for assistance.

When you are ready to go beyond the feeling of energy, ask for assistance. We are always ready to assist you. What is it that you want to do while you meditate? Picture it clearly in your mind, set this goal and ask for assistance, and we will be there for you. Remember that the path is not a smooth one. Sometimes you will be able to go forward at good speed, but sometimes you will be blocked in the same place for a while. This is the way it is. It is the way it is meant to be. If the path was a smooth one, you would not be able to process the amount of information coming to you and your engine would soon burn out. These stops, let's call them *rest stops,* are essential to your learning experience and your health.

In love and peace, thank you all for being here today.

I Have the Power in Me to Make It Happen

Knenesset, I have been feeling your energy on and off, but I could not bring myself to sit down and write. I am a bit sad today. As you know, tomorrow will be my last day here in this company and I will miss this office. Somehow I am extremely calm considering that I will be out of a job by tomorrow, but I cannot bring myself to be nervous. I do not know what is happening, but this time it is different from all the previous ones. I am ready to listen.

You are calm because you know that everything will be taken care of, responded Knenesset. You know that everything will sort itself out in the best possible way for you.

Dalende, all of you have the power to create your future according to your thoughts and feelings. The power comes from Source and you are part of Source. You are the only one limiting yourself; nobody is doing it to you. This limiting is not generated outside you but within you, by your thoughts, feelings, and emotions. You are doing it to yourself.

How can I change my way of thinking and feeling?

The only way is to be conscious at all times of what you think and feel and work at changing it. Live in the now at all times and you will achieve change. There is nothing else but the *now.* That is the only thing that exists.

Why do people get what they are afraid of? Because they spend their *nows* thinking about what they fear the most, and then they are surprised when their fears become reality. Whatever you think and fear the most, that is what you will get. It is your strongest probability for the next *now.* Concentrate on how you would like to live this now, right now. Think of only that. Feel it deep down inside of you. Extend this feeling into a subsequent now and that is how it goes. It will work. But you have to do it consciously. Do not let yourself be led astray. You need to focus on this and not give in to distractions.

You are showing some emotion, Knenesset. I did not know you could have emotions.

We all have emotions. I am only using emotion to make you understand in your terms what you can do. Imagine yourself *now* in the way you would like to live, and feel it. Feel it. Do not think about anything else. You will see how your reality will start to change. It has to. By law, it has to change. This is one of the great laws of this universe. You will become what you think and you will think what you want to become. It all starts in your thoughts, in the energy of your thoughts. Only you can decide what you want to become, and you will by the power of your thoughts. So watch what you think at all times. In every *now,* be aware of what you think, because you will see the manifestation when you believe it. *It is not "you will believe it when you see it," but "you will see it when you truly believe it."*

Think about this a moment. Make it your daily routine. Do not think about this sporadically, because it will not work. If you had a plant and you watered it one day all day and then left it without water for two weeks, and then decided to water it again for another day, do you think that that plant will thrive and grow? No, it will not. The same goes for your thoughts and desires. You might think about something you want all day long, but if you let that thought go without watering it for weeks on end, nothing is going to germinate from those thoughts. Remember this. Do not despair. There is no point in despairing. You have a very powerful mind. Use it!

In love and peace, thank you.

Chapter 5

Follow Your Intuition

Intuition is your link to Source. It is your link to your higher self. You all have intuition, but very few of you are tuned in to its frequency. You fill your brains with so many thoughts that you have no time left to listen to your intuition. In order to listen, you have to quiet down and know that the most important and larger part of you is inside, not outside. Your physical body is only the tip of the iceberg; the huge mass under the water is your spiritual body.

Intuition is not explainable because it cannot be quantified or defined. How would you define your intuition? The same as love, affection, fear, hate, and other emotions that are just accumulations of energy vibrating at different frequencies. It comes from deep inside you, usually in the form of a gut feeling. You should never question your intuition, because it is always right. Your intuition, the real intuition, the one coming from deep inside of you, without the interference of ego, is always right.

Sometimes intuition is mistaken for hope. Hoping for something is an ego-based emotion. When there is hope, there is also doubt. Hope and doubt go hand in hand. Faith comes from your higher self; where there is faith, there is no doubt. Faith is the knowing that something will take place, something that defies your ego that defies the laws of this physical plane. Faith cannot be quantified or defined. It just is. Intuition just is and it is always right. You have to keep the connection to the higher planes, the ones vibrating at a higher rate than yours, open if you want the information to flow. This takes conscious effort on your part. It takes effort and dedication, and living in the *now*. Always remember that only the now exists. There is nothing else. Now you are doing what you came here to do. You have started to write your book.

Intuition has been part of your life for a long time. It has always been with you. Intuition comes not only in the form of a hunch but also as dreams. Its purpose is to help you stay on the path you have set up for yourself before you reincarnated in this plane, and it can shed light on a difficult situation. When something is not for your *highest good*, you are shown the path to follow, sometimes through intuition or through your dreams. They are all linked. Life becomes easier when you learn to follow your intuition and know that this gut feeling is your best friend. Sometimes intuition can save you from a sudden death, or an accident or some unfortunate mistake that would only aggravate your present karma. It is your link to the rest of the dimensions that are all here with us at this moment.

So start your book by talking about intuition and how it shaped your life, because, if you analyze your life, you have always followed your intuition. And when you intentionally chose to ignore it, things stopped flowing in the right direction. You are all here to learn the lessons you have set up for yourselves, but some of you get lost in the many aspects of the learning and lose sight of the ultimate goal: the learning itself. Everything is an experience and it should be lived as such. It should be seen as such. Always look at your experiences and see the lessons in them. Look at what each experience is trying to tell you. Thanks to having followed your intuition, you are where you are today. By following your intuition, you are the person you are today. By following your intuition, you are on your path to Source. You still have a long road ahead of you, but you also have the satisfaction of knowing that you are on the right path and that there is so much more to this life than just living to pass the time until the end comes.

In love and peace, thank you.

What Exactly Is Intuition?

Knenesset, what exactly is intuition?

It is as part of you as any part of your physical body. Every day you go about your life without paying any attention to your physical organs. You do not think about your eyes, liver, spleen, brain, and heart during every minute of your day. You only focus on their function when they start to malfunction. The same works for intuition. Many of you live without even knowing what intuition is. Intuition cannot be defined in precise terms, nor can it be quantified. Can love be defined in precise terms? Can it be quantified? Each one of you has a different concept of love and its intensity. Every sentient being has a different view of love and how it affects their lives. Can hate, fear, and compassion be defined in precise terms? None of these feelings can. They are subjective to each one of you. What fear means to one person will mean something totally different to another. So why is intuition so important in your lives? Because your intuition links you to your higher self, and once you discover and use this link you will never be alone again.

You are not composed exclusively of physical matter. You are an amazing composition of physical, electrical, and spiritual matter. Whether you are a religious person or not, you will agree that you must have given some thought to the so-called afterlife. Once you are born, the next unavoidable event in your lives will be your death. Your parents use a lot of energy to get ready to receive you, to welcome you into this new reality. You all agree that the same energy is not present when you get ready to depart this reality. Everyone tries to ignore this certain event until it happens. You are born surrounded by people who love you and depart, most of the time, alone, with no loving faces around you. Why this inconsistency in your behavior? Why are you happy when you receive a new life and ignore the departure of a wise being? Because the new life will arrive in your present reality, into your world, and the wise life will depart toward the unknown, to a place you know nothing about. None of you have firsthand, exact information on life after your physical death. How do you know there will be a life after death? Nobody has come back to say so, and you have chosen to ignore death in the hope to make it disappear.

Life is everywhere. Scientists are just now discovering that there is no such thing as a void. Voids do not exist. Consciousness, intelligent consciousness, permeates everything, even what you used to call void. Physics tells you that nothing is wasted, that matter is always transformed into another element. You know that the physical components of your old bodies will be transformed into different elements that will become part of the earth and air. But what happens to your nonphysical side, that part that is in you but you cannot define because it cannot be detected and measured by the machines you have invented? What is life? Can anybody really define what it is that gives you life and once it is withdrawn takes life from you? You can only document the event and give some physical explanations on its cause, but you cannot really say why, at a precise moment, the life force that you cannot measure or define leaves your bodies.

Intuition is what links you to this life force. Intuition is what guides and protects you along the path you have chosen to live. Intuition is what will assist you in selecting the choices that will be best suited for learning the lessons you have set up for yourselves. Intuition will also protect you from experiences that will interfere with the learning that you are here to live. Intuition is a trusted guide. This is why it is vital to learn about intuition and how to access it during your lifetime. As I said, you can certainly live your life without being aware of your intuition, but if you learn to recognize and follow your intuition it will make your life so much more interesting, rewarding, and uncomplicated.

At present, most beings live in a vacuum. You are here on earth living a life that you know when it started but do not know when it will end, and for a great majority of beings a life that they firmly believe cannot be repeated. You just appear and then disappear again with no connections but the ones you have learned to acknowledge as your reality. We have learned that the space that appears *void* is no longer void, so why should your life be so disconnected from everything around it? Nothing on this plane is disconnected or separate from each other. You are all part of one another; you are all part of the same life force. You are just individual sparks of this life force. This life force is what runs through all your veins, through all your physical bodies. This life force is not mine, yours, or theirs. It belongs and is shared by all of us, regardless of color, religion, or type of creation through all dimensions. It is us. Intuition is part of this life force and as such is an integral part of us. You cannot be separate from your intuition, but most beings are usually unaware of its presence.

You become aware of your intuition only as a result of some serious experiences that happened in your lives. Problems and illnesses force us to look inside, and people usually have the most memorable experiences of their lives when they go through very difficult problems or face serious illnesses. At these moments, the reality they lived seems to change and a new reality sets is. They open up to their higher self. They become whole beings.

In love and peace, thank you.

Further Insight into Meditation and Brief Explanation on Linear Time

Knenesset, can you elaborate a bit more on the subject of meditation?

Yes. There are lots of stages to meditation. Learning to feel and use energy is just the first one. It is like learning how to walk when you are a baby. You are born a human being, but you have to learn to walk, speak, eat, fend for yourself, etc. Meditation takes you beyond the basic human being because it puts you in touch with the rest of you, *the expanded you,* where you have to learn to feel and use the energy that is part of you and connects you to everything that is. Do not be frustrated. You are doing very well, and you have come a long way since you became aware of this path. Everything has its time, and, just as babies do, you have to take one step at a time. The other doors will open one at a time when you are ready.

What you have to do now is to be conscious of your energy all the time, not just during meditation or at special times. Your energy is part of you at all times, and as you are aware of the functioning of your eyes, mouth, etc., you have to be aware of your energy. Remember that this energy is connecting you to everything that is. You are part of everything and everything is part of you. Once you do this, you will be able to feel the fluctuations in your energy field and interpret the cause of the changes. Always be aware of your energy and how it feels. Do this consciously. Do not leave it for special moments during meditation. It is part of you, and as such you should always be aware of it. What are you feeling right now?

I feel energy in my left fingers, and down my back.

Do you recognize this energy?

Is it yours or somebody else's? I think it is somebody else's.

What else do you feel? Is it a good energy?

Yes. I do not feel anything negative about it.

Always be conscious of what you feel and always be aware of the energy in you and around you. Everything has energy and very soon you should be able to feel it. Another important thing is not to forget to ask. Ask for the information you want to learn. Do not wait for me to select the lesson. If there is anything in particular you want to know about, ask me and I will try to teach you. If I cannot teach you, another teacher will step in and teach you as others have done in the past. Being a teacher does not mean I know everything, but I can certainly find out the right information for you and help you to complete your mission.

I understand. I am really interested in learning about time, about travel through time as we know it here on this plane. Does time exist in the other dimensions?

No, time does not exist the way you know it. Time is only a linear reference to be used on this plane. Everything on this plane has a beginning and an end. Every event has a beginning and an end in order to exist at that precise point. If you could not measure events, you would lose your sense of direction. You would not be able to precisely pinpoint an event that took place (past) or will take place (future). You could not tell when the event started or when it ended, when it will start or when it will end, or how long it lasted or will last. Events would stretch forever. This has to do with reincarnation. Time as it is conceived on this plane will allow you to view your lives as separate experiences even though they are not. You are at this moment the composite of the experiences you learned in all your lives. Your previous lives are all here with you right now. The Dalende you know is the sum of all the lives that you have had on this plane, both as female and male. You are the sum of all the experiences and the lessons you had to learn during those lives. If linear time did not exist, you would not be able to tell if the lives you lived happened prior to this one and in what order.

This is a very dense and orderly plane. Time exists to teach you to program the experiences you will have and to control the events in your life. It is also true, before you ask me, that you can travel through time to the past and to the future, for the simple reason that linear time does not exist anywhere else. Time is a series of pulses that are recorded as they are emitted by your thoughts and emotions. Everything that happens on this plane is recorded. Time is only one way to record events. Pulses are slightly different from energy. Pulses are more like bursts of energy. These bursts are recorded as such and they are easy to detect by the experienced time traveler. Energy fluctuates in waves; time pulses do not. They are bursts of energy. For example, when you interpret your Tarot cards, you are not exactly looking into the future but to the best probability for you in the future. The probability can change, because it will be affected by your thoughts and emotions. Let's say that you interpret a spread of cards as the death for somebody. This does not mean that the person is going to die; it only means there is a possibility that the person is going to die. If you tell the person that he or she is going to die in the near future, that probability might come true, because it will be activated by the thoughts of impending doom that the person will have. So you would have started a chain of events that would probably lead that person to his or her death. Time in itself does not exist. What give it life are your thoughts. Your thoughts have life and order. You think in a succession of images. This is what gives time its existence. Nothing else.

You mentioned that time is just a series of pulses that are recorded. Well, where are they recorded?

They are recorded in the energy grid surrounding the earth. Each body in space has its own energy grid. The purpose of these grids is to record the time pulses, because they will be used as reference by all sentient beings on this plane. The earth, as all other planets on this plane, is surrounded by energy grids that record the time pulses that will be reflected back to earth to create linear time, to keep the succession of events alive, so to speak, and to give consistency to this hologram that you are living in. Do you understand now?

Yes, a little bit better. Thank you for today's lesson.

In love and peace, thank you.

The Reason for Meditation

Let's talk about meditation.

Meditation is a window into a vast universe. It gives you the opportunity to travel to other dimensions and observe your plane from a wider perspective. Meditation is also used as a medical tool to achieve relaxation and cure anxiety. It has many other applications, but these are the most widely known at the moment in your plane.

Meditation is thinking with your higher being. Right now, you think with your mind. When you meditate, it is your higher being who thinks and directs your energies and images. Your chakras are the energy centers of your higher being, and it is with their use that you will be able to access the higher dimensions. They are the equivalent of your physical senses. Your physical senses are to be used for life on this plane, but the energy senses (chakras) are to be used when accessing the other dimensions. Your physical senses are not designed to sense the higher dimensions. They are not designed to feel and recognize energy.

Everything is energy and your chakras are the senses that will allow you to feel and work with the energies. Meditation is the tool that allows you to become aware of and feel your energy centers and helps them to expand. Once energy flows through all of your chakras, then you will start feeling and seeing things that you have never felt or seen before. A new world will come into focus, a world that contains everything. As I told you before, what you see with your physical senses is only the tip of the iceberg. The rest you will only be able to see by using the energy of your chakras. As somebody said, prayer is talking to God; meditation is listening to God. This is very true.

By God, we understand Source, the Creator of everything, Pure Conscious Energy. Pure Conscious Energy is everywhere and in everything, but your physical senses are not able to pick it up or comprehend the vastness of it all and its composition. This is why meditation is so very important. By meditating daily, you will be able to feel the energy and communicate with Source. At the same time, you will be giving your physical body a much needed rest. And by doing this, you will allow it to recuperate its balance. Haven't you noticed how you have not had a single cold or flu since you started to meditate regularly? Do you think this is just coincidence? No, it isn't. By meditating, you are balancing the energies in your body, and your energies flow smoothly without interruptions. These accumulations of energy, which interrupt the flow of energies in your physical body, are the cause of all the illnesses on this plane.

Meditation is an essential tool that should be used by everyone desiring to walk on the path of knowledge and health. It is more essential than any physical exercise. Excess of physical exercise, as is the fashion now, will in the long run injure your body. The body has not been designed for this type of daily abuse. Moderate exercise is fine and healthy, but excessive exercise with the only purpose to keep your body trim and fashionable is totally wrong. It will only wear your body down. Through meditation, you can heal your physical body. By channeling energy through your body and its components, you are ensuring your health. You can heal and revitalize every cell in your body through meditation. If there is one discipline that should be taught to every being on this plane, it is *meditation*. Meditation will not only heal your physical body but also connect you with Source and the rest of creation. It will make you *whole*.

In love and peace, thank you.

Have Faith in Yourself: Be the Captain of Your Boat

Knenesset, during the past two days I have not felt too well. Do you know what it was?

Your energies were out of balance, and they still are slightly. Keep on meditating every morning and evening. Try to bring your energy into your heart and then release it all around you. This should help you.

You must know that I have been a bit off because I have been without a job, and more than that because I have no faith in myself. Every time something unexpected happens in my life, my whole system falls apart and reverts to the familiar pattern of fear. This has been most frustrating. I thought I had improved a bit, but now I know that I am still far from achieving peace, love, and trust.

Dalende, do not judge yourself too harshly. Look at this as another lesson in your life, a lesson you need to learn in order to continue to walk on the long path to enlightenment. You know the path is long, difficult, and full of challenges. This is what makes you strong and, in the end, the reward is well worth all the efforts and sufferings. You also know that all the lessons you had to learn in your life were placed there for a purpose.

Your situation now is no different from the previous ones. It is just a lesson. I already told you many, many times that you will be fine, that you will be taken care of. You have a mission. Your main focus right now should be on fulfilling your mission.

This book needs to be written and soon—the sooner the better.

I know, but I am still a bit confused as to the way I should present this book to the public. I am not a born writer and this is not going to be an easy task for a mathematician.

I understand, but what you should do is write the same way you talk. Imagine yourself talking to a friend, a very good and trusted friend. What would you tell this friend? How would you talk to her? Remember this always and you will not fail. You cannot fail.

The subject should be your life and the way intuition has influenced it. Talk about the way you have learned to follow your intuition and the messages sent to you by us, your guides. Break the story down into short chapters. Do not get bogged down in details. There will be plenty of time afterward for you to explain the details. This first book should be short and concise. It should be in the form of a story to a friend.

Let's assume as an example that you will die shortly. What would you like your legacy to be? What will your contribution be to the beings sharing this lifetime with you? What would you like to tell them? This will be the subject of your book, a farewell letter to a friend. Now that you have the idea of what we want, the rest should come more easily. Dalende, you have tremendous abilities, but you still lack confidence in yourself. Why is that?

You still feel separate from Source. You still feel as an individual separate from the rest. This has to change. You are linked to all and everything that is. You are part of everything there is. Everything is part of you and you are nothing more than a reflection of the rest. You are a reflection of your parents, your environment, and all the thoughts you have had in your life until now. This is who you are. These thoughts have defined you. You have not defined your thoughts. You have been like a boat floating in the middle of rough seas, tossed around by the waves, without a destination. You have not mapped out your course toward the port where you want to go, but you have let the currents toss you around and you have only survived. You have not been the captain of your ship, but you have been at the mercy of your ship. When will you take charge of your boat? What are you waiting for? You have been given many opportunities and lessons. You just have to learn them and follow them. This is all it takes.

The good thing now is that you know that you should behave differently, that you should face life and your lessons in a different way. You know that you should not give in to fear. You know there is an alternative way of doing and thinking. This is awareness. You have reached the point where you are aware of the alternative. You can now exercise your free will. You can either stay in fear or walk into the light. The choice is up to you. Why would you stay in fear? You have chosen this path many times before and it has led you nowhere. Why don't you try something else as an experiment? Try to change your thoughts, one by one, and see where it leads you. Be the captain of your boat. This is the meaning of this lesson, to teach you to have faith in yourself. It is going to be hard, especially after doing and thinking the same things for years on end. Change will not be easy, but you have the strength and the knowledge to do it. Start right now.

In love and peace, thank you.

Short Lesson on the Meaning and Use of the Merkaba

I have been reading about the Merkaba and frankly I do not understand how to activate it. I think I know what it is for, but why do you have to go through the process of counting your breaths?

It is through the breath that you activate your energy system. Each group of breaths activates different energy coordinates. The activation of the Merkaba is not a procedure that should be taken lightly. Once activated, the Merkaba will allow you to travel through all the existing dimensions and through time, and you will become an interdimensional traveler. The reason why you should not use the Merkaba without assistance is because you will not be able to understand everything you see in the other dimensions, and most importantly your energy field needs to be compatible with the one of the dimension you visit. So it is not a procedure that I would recommend for common use as there will be consequences to your being if your energy field vibrates at a different frequency than it should.

You need to learn about dimensions and time before you are ready to activate your Merkaba. Actually, the Merkaba is not exactly a vehicle but more an energy field that will help you to integrate with Spirit. Once you are integrated with Spirit, you will be able to be everywhere at all times. Since your body will have to adapt to the high energy level, you should do it only under the guidance and the authorization of your guides.

In love and peace, thank you.

Lessons from Ego and the Importance of Clear Ideas

Dalende, I know we have talked about this subject before, but we have to revisit it once again to make sure that what you need to learn is very clear and there is no confusion possible.

By now, it should be quite clear to you that this plane is nothing more than a holographic plane where you create the experiences you live. You hold the power to create your experiences; nobody else does. If you surrender your power to outside sources, you will never achieve what you want. So far, we have established two facts: that you hold the power to make things happen as you would like them to happen and that you must have a clear idea of what you want. I would suggest you work on these two issues before you proceed. Dedicate some time to these, either through meditation or just letting yourself think with your heart, not your head, or any preconceived ideas, but with your heart.

Your connection to your higher self is through your heart. Do you remember the picture of the Sacred Heart of Jesus? The connection is in the heart. Love, intuition, and a whole series of wonderful, altruistic feelings are based in the heart. You have to learn to think with your heart, not your head. The thoughts generated in your head are ego based; the ones generated or felt in your heart are love based. Do not let yourself be guided by what your brain tells you can be done or how it should be done, but be guided by your heart. What you feel in your heart at this moment is what is right for you.

There is a task that needs to be completed before we continue, and you have been trying to avoid it at all costs. Write down what you want, what you feel in your heart is right for you. Do not give in to any ideas as to why this cannot be done. Do not give in to your ego. Always remember that you are the creator of your own world. Nobody else is.

Ego is in a way the Devil depicted by the Christian churches. If you think of the episode of Adam and Eve, and the snake and the apple, what does it remind you of? They were living happily in a wonderful paradise where all their needs were met, but this was not enough. They were tempted by the only fruit that was forbidden to them; they already had everything but this fruit. It was not the fruit itself but what it represented. It represented the only thing that they could not have and this temptation became the most important wish in their peaceful existence. They became so obsessed by it that they finally gave in to temptation and their whole world changed.

Naturally, this is just a metaphor. Even if man had everything available to him to live a peaceful and satisfied existence, his ego would step in and lead him into temptation. Ego is only exercising its own nature: control. Ego always wants to be in control, and it will persist until it obtains control. Ego is temptation. Ego leads beings deep into materialism because ego belongs to this plane. It is alive in this plane and it is the master of this plane. Ego does not exist anywhere else. Ego will always try to draw your attention so that it can justify its existence.

Ego lives through you and through your thoughts. Don't you see its game? Look around you. Do you see people who can rightly say that they are totally satisfied with their way of life, with what they have? No, you will see people who are always complaining about millions of things that they see as being wrong in their lives. You will see people accumulating and hoarding possessions at an alarming rate. They will go on accumulating and hoarding during their whole lives, even if they know very well that they will not have enough time to use all their possessions, even if they know they will not be able to use all the money they have accumulated. Why? Because it makes them feel powerful and in control. But what are they in control of? They will have to die someday and will not be able to take anything with them.

Ego is always there by their side, tempting them with the desire for more and more (the proverbial red apple), even when it is not humanly possible for them to use everything they have accumulated already. So who is in control of their lives? Ego or them? *Ego.* Ego will always be in control, because ego is what makes them feel powerful and important. They live by what their egos dictate, not by what they feel is right in their hearts. The lesson on this plane is to transcend ego, because you have to transcend it to realize your unity with Source. You have to consciously renounce your ego if you want to reach enlightenment and graduate from this school.

Do you understand now? Start with a blank slate, as if you had just been born, and look at yourself from your heart. How do you see your life? What would you like to see happen in your life? How would you like to live your life? Be frank with yourself. Do not judge yourself, and, most important of all, remember that you are the Creator of your own life and you bear the sole responsibility for your creations. It is not good blaming others, as so many sentient beings routinely do in your plane, for the results of their actions. The responsibility is entirely yours, and when you pass on to the next plane, you will have to answer for all your thoughts and actions, and there is no harsher judge than yourself. Believe me.

Dalende, it is time for you to look at yourself as a wonderful sentient being. You are a wonderful being. Forget about all the ideas that were placed in your head by your family and society. Start anew with the ideas you feel are right for you in your own heart. Whatever you feel is right for you, that is the path to follow in this lifetime.

In love and peace, thank you.

Defining Your Needs and Asking for What You Desire

Knenesset, I was reading something this morning that I did not understand. Why can we materialize all sorts of physical things, as cars, houses, furniture, etc. and not be able to materialize money, physical bills as such? The author of the book I was reading said that this cannot be done, and frankly I do not understand why, since money is energy and the bills are certainly physical. Is there a law against this? Could you please explain it to me?

Dalende, the author is not entirely correct. Actually, there is no law against manifesting the physical bills you call money. As you say, they are energy, and as such they should be treated the same as the rest of the physical things in your plane. In order to manifest physical bills, you must have a very clear idea of how many, of what denominations, of what currency, and for what purpose. What happens with money is that it is usually used to purchase a series of things, so there is a natural association between money and the articles you desire to have. It is easier to think of the article, because it can manifest in your life in many different ways, and not necessarily through the use of money, because you are open to creativity.

Money, as such, would only be used to save it in your bank account or to purchase items you need, or to donate to different people and causes. How much do you feel you need to have in your bank account? Will a certain amount of money in your account make you happy? Will it give you peace of mind? Have you really explored the feeling behind your desire to have money in your bank account? I would suggest you do this as a first step.

The two feelings that come to my mind are peace of mind and freedom to do the things I want to do. I do not wish to continue to see a job, any job, as the only way to manifest money in my life. I would like to be creative and open up to the energy of Source. I would like to be able to trust Source in all areas of my life. I would like to get rid of the fear I have always carried with me throughout this lifetime.

You are already doing it. By recognizing the source of the problem, you are effectively working toward getting rid of your fears. Acknowledgement and acceptance will help you to erase the fear you have lived by. Expand your thoughts on this subject.

So far, your life has been defined by very narrow thoughts, and you have lived in accordance to those thoughts. You have repeatedly said that you are not creative, that you do not want to work anymore, that you want to stay at home, and that you have achieved what you wanted; the company you were working for closed down and you were left without a job. You forgot to include in this picture how you wanted to stay at home and what it meant for you not to work in an office anymore. You forgot to give your subconscious the parameters for this picture. Let's do it now. Give this picture some thought. You are an excellent analyst so use this skill. Analyze this picture and see what is missing.

I know what is missing. I did not include how I would see myself living without working at a regular job. I just expressed my feelings and assumed that my subconscious knew how to make it happen in the best possible way for me.

Dalende, remember that the subconscious is the equivalent of your present-day computers. It is a computer that works with pure energy and thought energy. It is extremely advanced, but it still needs accurate and very detailed information to process your request and to achieve your desired outcome. If you omit some details, the outcome will not be the one you desire because the formula you are using is not complete.

Stop talking for the sake of talking and only say the words you really mean to say. You should write down in a journal everything you say and then look at the events happening in your life, and you will see how everything you express becomes manifest. Let's do this. Look at your life now. Write down everything and remember the words you said in the past year and see if the situation you are living at present was shaped by the words you said. You should recognize the cause.

Energy needs to manifest, as this is its purpose. Everything is a manifestation of energy; everything is energy. Thoughts are energy and your emotions and words give them life in the physical. I am here to help and assist you, but there is some work you need to do in order to progress on this path. You are doing great. Do not worry. I will keep my promise of assistance. Remember that one other important thing is to ask, and you never ask. You assume that everything you think and keep inside of you is automatically heard and answered. This is not so. The power of the spoken word is great, very great. If I am with you, I can see your thoughts quite easily, but if I am not with you at any given moment, you can reach me through the spoken word. The vibrations caused by the spoken word can be felt and seen from far away. They are like ripples in a pond. So remember to speak out loud when you need something and the answer will come. It has to come. This is the law. No request can go unanswered.

In love and peace, thank you.

The Realization That You Are the Master of Your Life

I have shaped my life with my thoughts. This is what I have learned so far. I have selected my experiences with my thoughts. I have nobody to blame but myself. I have also had a lot of help, guidance, and protection in my life, and I am thankful for that. The realization that one can shape life with his or her own thoughts is a very powerful tool. Once you come to this realization, your whole approach to life changes and nothing can continue to be the same. You hold the power of the rest of your life in your hands. You hold the power to live your life the way you think it is right for you and for your highest good. We are co-creators with Source, and in this respect we are very much like Him/Her.

What have I created in my life? Who I am, how I live, my experiences, and my fights—every single experience was created in my mind first, through my thoughts. I am not a ship in the middle of the sea, but I am the captain of my ship. This is a powerful realization. I have to thank my teacher, my guardian angel, and all my guides for this powerful realization. You have made this possible for me. Without your gentle prodding and support, I would have never reached this point in my life. I would have never come to this realization. I am the master of my own life. Amazing!

At this point in my life, I am exactly where I thought I would be, and where I have thought myself to be. My thoughts, my beliefs, and my fears have all guided me to this point. I am now living in the States, thanks to the intervention of my teacher and my guides who have helped me to face and heal some very deep wounds from the past. I know that I am here on a mission that needs to be accomplished before my final departure or graduation. This part of my life needs to be lived in this country, and I am here to heal myself and others.

The question is this: What do I want to do now? Where do I want to go? How do I plan to get there? This is what I have to think about. I have to create the right thoughts and emotions so that my subconscious can create exactly what I want. Let's think about this a while. What do I want? I want a different life style. How exactly different? What do I mean by different? I want to be free to do what I want, when I want. I do not want to be bound by thoughts of lack.

I know that I still have a lot of work to do if I want my desires to become reality, but I consider this only the beginning. I have jotted down these desires and they need to be expanded to create the reality I want for myself. So my work right now is to create the thoughts that will manifest the life that I see myself living. I need to really work on the details of this picture if I want to achieve what I desire in the way I desire.

Thank you for your inspiration.

In love and peace.

Knenesset's Origin and How We Should Think

Knenesset, I would like to talk about you today and how you decided to get in touch with me. You told me that you belong to the tribe of Elohim and you come from Ursus. I had never heard of the name before. Where exactly is Ursus?

It is a large planet in another galaxy, far removed from earth, he responded.

How is life in your planet?

It is very similar to the one on earth. The only difference is our lack of individuality, in contrast to what you have here. We have always been more united than you are here and we work for many common goals and for the benefit of our entire race. The similarity between our two planets is the reason of my assignment to earth and its inhabitants. I do not reincarnate anymore because I have selected this way of service to other beings.

How do you decide with whom and when to connect?

That is decided by your energy levels. The type of energy you emit determines if I can get in contact with you or not. You all emit energy at all times, and the specific level of your energy is what attracts us to you. When your energy reaches a certain level, a channel of communication opens and makes you receptive to communication. It works in a way that is similar to your radio and TV transmissions. If you know the frequency, then you can tune in the same frequency and share the same communication channel. At this moment, you and I are sharing the same communication channel. You are receiving not only from me but from others also, some of whom you have already communicated with. As you progress in your meditation and your rate of vibration increases, you will receive from other beings as well, since you will be sharing a communication frequency with them. We are all here, learning with you and guiding you, just waiting to be of assistance. In order to be of assistance, we need to vibrate at the same frequency, otherwise, you would not be able to tune in and no communication would be possible.

97

Dalende, this is the way I chose to be of service. There are many of us sharing this plane with you. Many of you cannot see or hear us because there are very few of you vibrating at the same frequency we are. Your perception of this plane is tridimensional, but your plane is not really tridimensional. It comprises many dimensions, but your physical limitations are such that you are not able to perceive them all. As your vibration increases, your ability to see and hear will expand and your perception of your tridimensional world will change to encompass these new dimensions.

Ever since you were born, you have instinctively known that there were other *things* out there. Your most developed abilities have been your ability to dream the future and telepathy. You have been *guided* to where you are now. The difference between you and other sentient beings has been that you have always paid attention to this guidance and they have not. You have always accepted our presence, our guidance, and your *gifts* as something natural, something that originated deep inside you. You have been very fortunate in having parents who have always encouraged this side of you and accepted it as well. They never forced you to abandon your gifts.

When you dream your future, I would like you to understand that the future we are presenting you is not set in stone; it is only the highest probability. Your thoughts can influence the outcome of that probability. This is why people should not have their future read, especially highly impressionable beings, because it is presented to them as a definite outcome when it is only a probability. The problem arises when people focus their thoughts on this probable outcome, because then this probable outcome will become their future. Always remember that you are the creator of your own future and only you can determine what lessons you would like to learn and how to live them. You can find all the answers inside you. You do not need to empower anybody outside you to tell you what will happen in your life.

All the events that will happen in your life are the ones you have focused your attention on for a long time. If you want to change your future, just change your thoughts, which will change your vibrations and everything will have to change. That is the law. This is the famous law of the alchemists. You can transform the metals in your life to precious gold with your thoughts.

You have to know that, in order to manifest, you have to keep these thoughts alive in you for a certain period of time. There cannot be fluctuations to your creative energy if you want to manifest. Fluctuations mean surges or changes in your energy. In other words, the flow of your energy has to be kept stable with no surges or negative thoughts canceling your energy output. What humans do all the time is cancel their original energy output. They keep their energies fluctuating all the time, and then they wonder why their wishes do not come true.

A human life needs nine months to come to full manifestation, and the process of gestation has to be smooth, without any stresses, for it to come to a successful completion. The same applies to thoughts. Your thoughts are alive, full of energy, but in a form not yet manifested. They are the seeds of your life, full of potential probabilities. A thought needs steady energy and time to manifest. Any fluctuation will change its energy and nothing will be manifested. Your thoughts can be compared to a twister moving erratically at high speed over a landscape. Nobody controls the path of a twister and you certainly do not seem able to control the path of your thoughts. If you did, this plane would be a much better place to live.

You can control the path of your thoughts, since you are their creator. But before you can achieve this control, you have to decide which path to follow. This is why it is imperative for you to have a vision of a path and live in the *now*, always in the now. It is only when you live in the now that you are truly focusing on your thoughts at that precise moment. Your future is made up of a series of *nows*. This is the only way to manifest what you desire. Keep focusing on the now and everything you desire will come to be. Keep your energy flow steady and you will manifest your desires.

Each thought contains the essence of its potentiality, of what it intends to be, just like the seed contains the potential of a beautiful tree. The seed needs optimal conditions, such as water, soil, air, and sun, to grow and become the tree that it is intended to become. Thoughts also need the same optimal conditions to manifest. They need a steady input of high energy (a flow of constant, steady, nonfluctuating energy). This is why you need a crystal-clear idea of what you want to manifest. If you do not have a crystal-clear idea, then you will not manifest what you want but only the confused bits and pieces of a chaotic idea. This is why there is so much turmoil and confusion in your world. Confusion is the manifestation generated by incomplete and not well-defined thoughts and ideas.

In love and peace, thank you.

Chapter 6

Lessons Learned

I have been reading a book about these beings from the low fourth dimension that are here on earth right now trying to control everybody and everything. The idea is not shocking per se; I have been thinking and feeling for a long, long time that there is a ruling group behind the people we have elected for office. Their agenda seems to be to unite the whole world under one flag, so they can reap the maximum profits from this situation. What is still unclear to me is if they are beings from the fourth dimension or if they are from this dimension, just mortals who have been carried away by greed and the thirst for power. In a way, they have let their worst demons loose, and these demons have grown to the point where they completely dominate them.

Something the author said makes a lot of sense. If we look at the experiences we have had in our lives, we can see how we really think. It would be like looking at yourself in the mirror. Once you do this, you have a pretty good idea of how your subconscious operates. This concept became clear to me one night while I was watching a program of an inmate in a U.S. prison who had killed his first family and had been sentenced to a mental institution. As it turns out, this person had killed by mistake in Vietnam, during the Vietnam War, a mother and her four children. He kept on reliving this event in his mind every day of his life because he could not forgive himself for his senseless killing. Once free, he remarried, and again he killed his wife and child.

What does this tell you?

He was setting the stage again and again so he could be punished for what he did so many years ago in Vietnam, hoping that the punishment would set him free from his guilt.

Let's look at our lives and take a moment to observe the stages we prepare for our plays. Let's look at the scenes that repeat themselves time and time again and try to analyze them. If we do this, we will have the answer on the lesson that we are here to learn and we are desperately looking for. *This sounds easy to do, but, in reality, looking at ourselves from a detached point of view is quite difficult. We have to look at ourselves without letting our ego interfere in this process or the picture we get will be blurred. So look carefully at what it is that you keep doing time after time in your life.*

I keep on repeating the pattern I learned during my years with my family. I keep on setting the same stage. I keep on reliving the ideas my parents had. I have always denied myself the opportunity of expressing my creativity and my own ideas about life, the same ideas that have been part of me for so long. I have denied myself access to my subconscious, to all the experiences and lessons that I have learned through so many lifetimes. This is so amazing! I instinctively know that life should be different from the way the majority of us live it. I instinctively know that the physical and spiritual should go hand in hand to create balance in our lives.

The most important lessons in our lives are not learned in school or college. They are learned by living them. I know that this subject is not taught anywhere on this planet. It is only taught inside us by our higher self. The only way to find out if I am on the right track is to do a little experiment and see what the result is. If I am right, then I will have learned the main lesson in my life: how to live my life. Not only that, but I will have learned how to set up the stage for how I want to live my life and how to engage the help of my subconscious in this quest.

Always pay special attention to your thoughts because they set the stage for the play you want to live. Remember that the subconscious only executes. It does not have any discernment of its own, and you do. A computer (your subconscious) can only execute a program based on what the programmer (you) has created. The computer does not have the ability to tell you if the program you wrote is good or bad. It can only execute your commands and come up with the final product. There are no emotions involved, only precise commands (your thoughts).

Now the next step for me is to look at the stages I have set up repeatedly and analyze what the lesson is that I so desperately need to learn. Once this is done, then I will be able to set up a new stage based on how I see myself living my life now.

In love and peace, thank you.

Epilogue

My life, so far, has been a wonderful adventure. I have not always felt this way, but I have had tremendous help all these years. My guides have taken care of me with such patience and determination that I want to write this book to give thanks to all the wonderful guides who are accompanying me in this present journey. It has taken me many years of interpreting my dreams, searching for answers, reading about other people's experiences, crying, and despair to get to where I am today. This has not been an easy journey, and I am still on the path to a destination that it is not within my reach yet, but I have been instructed to share my experiences with you, my children, so you may recognize what is happening to you, and understand what you need to do to change your life.

I had always been a girl who was different from the rest. I had prophetic dreams, I was telepathic, and I had a yearning to find out more about our life on this planet. I was instinctively attracted to the Chinese, Japanese, Tibetan, and Egyptian cultures without even knowing why. I had never been to those countries and I was too young to have read books about them, but they were somehow familiar to me. Princes and princesses and Japanese samurais attracted me, and I made up my own personal stories where I invariably played the role of a princess. I have to thank my parents for letting me express my fantasies. They never scolded me, and my mother in particular was always there ready to listen to my *strange* dreams. As I grew up, my experiences intensified to the point where I had some prophetic dreams that included both family members and government personalities.

One afternoon, while I was taking a nap, I had a dream in which I was dying. I could not scream for help, and the certainty of death was so overwhelming that I just started praying and thinking about God, because I knew I was dying. Well, the next day we received news that one of my uncles had died while taking a nap. He had gone to bed to rest and never woke up. You may call it coincidence, but these dreams kept on happening at irregular intervals. They seemed to happen only when there was an event in the future that in some way would affect my life.

These dreams can happen to many of you. They are the language of the subconscious and the vehicle used by your guides. When communication cannot happen in any other way, they will send you a dream to warn you of impending danger, a particular situation that could affect your life, or a solution to a problem that has been troubling you. Dreams use a language of images that can be easily understood by you. Sometimes they are a bit scary, but if you write them down in a journal, you will soon decipher their code.

In my case, they always use water and animals to warn me of difficult situations I will face if I don't change my way of thinking. We get stuck in our ideas and emotions until they become so familiar that we cannot conceive any new ideas and we cannot let go of our emotions. This is our familiar ground, one we feel comfortable in, one that we know (or so we think) how to handle. Most of the times, these familiar ideas and emotions will lead us straight into disaster. Dreams are usually a warning sent to us to force us to change our familiar ways, because our persistence on the same path will only lead us to more problems and pain. It took me years to decipher the meaning of all these messages and to find out that a force I knew nothing about was at work. This force was my intuition.

I grew up thinking that we are alone on this one journey. We seem to appear on earth and then disappear again in the blink of an eye. Many religions tell us that this is just one event and that, depending on how we behave and do during this one event, we will gain our right to go to paradise or live in eternal hell. This definition never made much sense to me. I have a mathematical mind and the thought that the few years we live here on earth would determine my eternal future has always seemed totally unreasonable. Some people do not even get to live consciously until they reach full consciousness of their acts (usually at eighteen to twenty years of age). Do these people forfeit their right to eternal happiness if they die before eighteen to twenty? And what are seventy to eighty years in comparison to all eternity? Nothing. Just a speck in the immense frame of eternity. Many times, I also questioned what happened to all those sentient beings that killed so many in the name of their gods. Did they really think they were going to be awarded eternity in heaven for killing so many of their fellow beings? What had happened to the commandment "You shall not kill"?

We have many lives, not just one. We have many lessons to learn, and it is not humanly possible to learn them all in just a few years of conscious presence on this earth.

In love and light, thank you.

To be continued ...

A Final Thought

To know men is to be wise,
To know yourself is to be illuminated,
To conquer men is to have strength,
To conquer yourself is to be even stronger.
Tao Te Ching

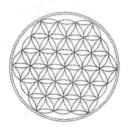

About the Author

Gelma Bruce currently lives in Greensboro, North Carolina. She began her spiritual journey during this life at the age of eight. In later years, she read the works of Emmet Fox, Bride Murphy, Edgar Cayce, Madame Blavatsky, *The Kybalion, The Children of the Law of One & the Lost Teachings of Atlantis,* and many other spiritual works. Gelma is an ordinary person who has lived an extraordinary life. She has always lived by her inner voice and prophetic dreams, and this is what has made all the difference. Gelma has had two teachers in her life: one physical and one nonphysical. She is most grateful to both for the lessons transmitted to her and for showing her how much more there is to life than the three dimensions we are so accustomed to.

A spiritual teacher and channeler, Gelma has been working with her guide, Knenesset, from the tribe of Elohim, since 2001. Dalende is the name the author works under when channeling with her guides. She gives talks based on her channeled messages.

The lessons presented in this book are the result of her channeling. Gelma now passes on these lessons to both of her children, who were also fortunate to have been born with their mother's amazing gift, and to you, the reader of this work. Check her website for more information: http://www.keytoyour-life.com.